In Pursuit of God

How do we pursue a deeper walk with God?

How do we keep our eyes focused on His ways?

How do we continue to observe faithfully His truths in an increasingly hostile world?

The answer, writes Ron Bridges, begins in the heart—the very center of our being, the home of our deepest intentions, the seat of our emotions.

The heart is the driving force in our lives. It is the place where we can most closely sense the character and reality of God.

If your heart desires a powerful, satisfying and intimate relationship with God, read on . . .

Also by Ron Bridges

Rediscovering Your First Love:
The Joys of a Devoted Heart

DISCIPLINES OF THE DEVOTED HEART

RONALD F BRIDGES

Here's Life Publishers

First Printing, October 1991

Published by
HERE'S LIFE PUBLISHERS, INC.
P. O. Box 1576
San Bernardino, CA 92402

Library of Congress Cataloging-in-Publication Data
Bridges, Ronald F.
    Disciplines of the devoted heart / Ronald F. Bridges.
        p.   cm.
    ISBN 0-89840-330-8
    1. Spiritual life. I. Title.
BV4501.2.B7243   1991
248.4—dc20   91-24693
                                        CIP

Unless indicated otherwise, Scripture quotations are from *The New American Standard Bible,* © The Lockman Foundation 1960, 1962, 1963, 1968, 1971, 1972, 1975, 1977.
Scripture quotations designated KJV are from the *King James Version.*
Scripture quotations designated NIV are from *The Holy Bible: New International Version,* © 1973, 1978, 1984 by the International Bible Society. Published by Zondervan Bible Publishers, Grand Rapids, Michigan.
Scripture quotations designated TLB are from *The Living Bible,* © 1971 by Tyndale House Publishers, Wheaton, Illinois.

Cover design by Cornerstone Graphics

For More Information, Write:
L.I.F.E.—P.O. Box A399, Sydney South 2000, Australia
Campus Crusade for Christ of Canada—Box 300, Vancouver, B.C., V6C 2X3, Canada
Campus Crusade for Christ—Pearl Assurance House, 4 Temple Row, Birmingham, B2 5HG, England
Lay Institute for Evangelism—P.O. Box 8786, Auckland 3, New Zealand
Campus Crusade for Christ—P.O. Box 240, Raffles City Post Office, Singapore 9117
Great Commission Movement of Nigeria—P.O. Box 500, Jos, Plateau State Nigeria, West Africa
Campus Crusade for Christ International—Arrowhead Springs, San Bernardino, CA 92414, U.S.A.

To my four special little gifts from God,
My beloved children,
Ryan, Tyler, Bethany and Kyle.

Your joy and endless enthusiasm has filled
our lives with a tremendous sense of
God's grace, mercy and love.

Contents

Part I

Stepping Up to the Starting Line

1

Your Spiritual Growth: Stalled, Sterile or Steady?

In all your ways acknowledge Him,
and He will make your paths straight
(Proverbs 3:6).

Continental Express flight #2286 was on its final approach into the Durango Airport when suddenly and without warning, everything and everyone in the plane were tumbling upside down. A few moments later, the plane crashed onto a field of trees and shrubs, waist-deep in snow. After the impact, nine survivors managed to escape through a gaping hole in the plane's fuselage. They huddled outside together under a constant snow-fall.

Peter Schauer, one of the least injured, decided to go for help. About an hour and a mile and a half later, he came to a highway and flagged down the first car to come by. He explained to the two women in the car that there had been a plane crash. Though he was bleeding and obviously exhausted, the women refused to let him into their car and told him to walk to a nearby farmhouse.

They added that they would drive to the next town and alert the authorities.

After finding the farmhouse, Schauer was forced to stand outside in the cold while an elderly lady resident pondered the sincerity of his story. Finally, after convincing her to call the authorities, he was allowed in to sit by the fire. He was later met by the sheriff and taken to the hospital. Fortunately, the remaining survivors were also rescued and taken to the hospital.

After reading this story, my first thought was, *How could people be so insensitive and uncaring?* But on second thought, I wondered what my reaction would be if I were traveling on a lonely stretch of mountain road and suddenly a ragged, middle-aged man appeared in the light of my car headlamps, waving his arms for me to stop. On the one hand, I would want to help this stranger in need, but on the other, I would have to wonder if the man was sincere or considering a criminal act.

Have you noticed that in this day and age it is becoming more and more difficult to discern the true intentions of people? A political leader running for public office promotes himself as being dignified, ethical and above reproach. He claims to conduct his life according to Christian values. Yet his every action is controlled by ulterior motives designed to feed his egocentric character by furthering his sphere of influence and control.

A mass-media evangelist preaches great moral, biblical truths and persuades thousands and thousands of believers with his "spiritual sincerity" to walk the straight and narrow. All the while, though, he is dabbling in gross sin.

And closer to home, two believers perform a similar function within a church or Christian organization. They both exhibit great spiritual piety. Yet one of them is failing miserably in his duties to his family, neglecting one of the most important responsibilities God has given him.

Are these examples merely a result of a few bad apples upsetting the apple cart? Or are they the products of the depraved state of man? The Bible clearly indicates that all of us, because of our sin nature, are prone to unrighteous behavior.[1] Solomon writes in the book of Ecclesiastes that "the hearts of the sons of men are full of evil" (9:3). The prophet Jeremiah proclaimed that the heart of man is more deceitful than anything else (Jeremiah 17:9). And Jesus affirmed to the disciples the very truth of this matter in no uncertain terms:

> That which proceeds out of the man, that is what defiles the man. For from within, out of the heart of men, proceed the evil thoughts, fornications, thefts, murders, adulteries, deeds of coveting and wickedness, as well as deceit, sensuality, envy, slander, pride and foolishness. All these evil things proceed from within and defile the man (Mark 7:20-23).

Man has a natural propensity to sin. Keeping that fact in mind, I've written this book to help you evaluate and enhance your spiritual condition in Christ according to necessary biblical guidelines. I want to challenge you to maintain a consistent level of growth by focusing on spiritual maturity in Christ. And I hope you will feel compelled to establish a pattern for growth that will endure through all circumstances, making you a shining trophy of God's immense love and grace to all the world, proving that victorious Pauline statement: "I can do all things through Him who strengthens me" (Philippians 4:13). I hope you will take this message seriously so that you can fully understand what it means to say, "I press on toward the goal for the prize of the upward call of God in Christ Jesus" (Philippians 3:14).

Though spiritual growth may seem subjective to

some people, Scripture contains several examples and standards by which we can effectively and practically judge our present condition in Christ. Throughout this book we'll evaluate the circumstances and experiences of many Bible characters as well as several key historical situations, studying both the victories and the failures. But before we get to that, it is important that we understand the difference between our *condition* in Christ and our *position* in Christ.

Our Condition in Christ

Perhaps one of the greatest books penned by the apostle Paul is the book of Philippians. Though he was about sixty-one years old and in a prison cell in Rome, he writes like a young man of twenty just home from his honeymoon. His joy and contentment are clearly overflowing throughout the pages of this great little book.

How could Paul express such an attitude while being chained to a prison guard? He had confidence in his *position* in Christ. Despite his physical circumstances, he could say without hesitation, "For I am confident of this very thing, that He who began a good work in you will perfect it until the day of Jesus Christ" (Philippians 1:6). In regard to his imprisonment he could say with great confidence:

> For I know that this shall turn out for my deliverance through your prayers and the provision of the Spirit of Jesus Christ, according to my earnest expectation and hope, that I shall not be put to shame in anything, but that with all boldness, Christ shall even now, as always, be exalted in my body, whether by life or by death (Philippians 1:19,20).

You see, Paul had such confidence in his position in Christ that his condition in Christ (his walk with the Lord) was continually being strengthened. This allowed him to make such bold statements as, "I shall not be put to shame in anything" (1:20) and, "Christ shall . . . be exalted in my body, whether by life or by death" (1:20).

Our condition in Christ (our current level of spiritual maturity) will be affected by our understanding of our position in Christ (our salvation).

If you are at all unsure of your salvation in Jesus Christ, then your relationship with Him will most likely reflect a lack of confidence—a spiritual immaturity. In such a condition, any spiritual growth will lose its strength with each new trial or temptation.

Non-Fat Christianity

But what about the believer who is secure in his position in Christ, yet shows no evidence of spiritual maturity beyond the new birth? Or what about the believer who is secure, but frequently feels stalled in his spiritual life?

Any number of things could contribute to one or both of these conditions. But I've noticed one major reason for a lack of growth in the Christian's life: A believer enjoys the "fat" of the milk of God's Word too much to move on to the "meat." Let me explain.

The apostle Peter describes a process of spiritual growth using the analogy of a new baby's instinctive yearning for his mother's pure milk. Peter stressed to the believers of his day that they must yearn for the *pure* (*adolos*) milk of the Word of God:

> Therefore, rid yourselves of all malice and all deceit, hypocrisy, envy, and slander of every kind. Like newborn babies, crave the pure spiritual milk, so that by it you may grow up in your salvation, now that you have tasted that the Lord is good (1 Peter 2:1-3, NIV).

Notice how Peter specifically states that the milk of God's Word is *pure*. The adjective he chooses to describe this purity (*adolos*) is a term depicting something that is uncontaminated and free from any defilement. William Barclay further clarifies this distinction:

> *Adolos* is an almost technical word to describe corn that is entirely free from chaff or dust or useless or harmful matter. In all human wisdom there is some admixture of what is either useless or harmful; the Word of God alone is altogether good.[2]

Perhaps believers who are not spiritually growing are mixing the pure milk of the Word of God with the useless fat of man's wisdom. This creates a comfortable yet compromising mixture of God's truths and their own "knowledge." As a result, they wallow in a weakened spiritual condition which is neither challenging nor strengthening to their lives.

I believe the mixing of God's truths with man's wisdom is a principle cause for much of the spiritual immaturity seen in Christianity today. Too many believers live a type of spiritual schizophrenia: They fully recognize the power of God in one area of their life but totally trust in their own abilities in another area. I am reminded of our Lord's declaration to the disciples: "No servant can serve two masters; for either he will hate the one, and love the other, or else he will hold to one, and despise the other" (Luke 16:13).

Spiritual maturity has nothing to do with increasing our knowledge. Rather, true spiritual maturity results from a growing and consistent love and knowledge of God and His ways. Our daily spiritual diet must consist of time spent with Him and the pure milk of His Word. In turn, this leads us to His solid food and a greater understanding of His character (Hebrews 5:12-14).

Burning Out or Burning On

A few years ago, my wife Janet and I took up bicycling. We frequently enjoy this healthy outdoor activity together. In fact, I have grown to enjoy riding so much that I try to schedule time for lengthy rides in order to train for endurance events such as century (100 mile) and double century (200 mile) rides.

In preparing myself for such events, I have come to understand and value the importance of maintaining a properly balanced diet throughout my training. Altering my diet here and there greatly decreases my energy output and depletes my ability to ride at my best. This is especially evident when I am faced with a lengthy hill climb or a sudden sprint and I need to draw on my energy reserves. After all, my muscles can only respond according to what and how they have been fed.

This conditioning process is similar to our endurance in spiritual growth. A permanently maintained diet of God's Word along with consistent time alone with Him continually restores and strengthens our spiritual stamina. Our energy output will remain high and we'll be ready to respond to whatever life throws at us.

Many times, however, we alter our spiritual diet due to neglect. Because of busy schedules or simple laziness, we might go for days or weeks without spending any quality time with God or in His Word. If we're too busy, we will likely substitute and justify our "work" for Him as time spent with Him. Such behavior can only lead to spiritual burnout since our work for Him does not involve time spent abiding in Him and drawing on His power. Our work merely is a matter of the flesh drawing on its own finite energy. Subsequently, we soon lack the desire and drive to remain on the cutting edge of our Christian growth. We pull back from doing battle on the front lines. We withdraw into the pews and become selfish with our time and energy.

In the case of simple laziness, our motivation to grow is suppressed by a greater desire to fulfill our own personal wants and needs before we surrender our time and effort to God and His desires.

In either case, our reservoir of spiritual stamina has not been replenished because we have either limited or cut off the source of our spiritual nourishment. We have neglected our personal walk with the Lord who is our bread of life and fountainhead of living water (John 6:35; 7:37,38).

How can we ever expect to grow in the Christian life without abiding in Christ? Jesus made it very clear to His disciples: "I am the vine, you are the branches; he who abides in Me, and I in him, he bears much fruit; for apart from Me you can do nothing" (John 15:5).

Abiding in Christ means that we live with a constant awareness of His presence. His truths permeate our thinking. His love directs our motives. And His life becomes exemplified in our daily walk. Then, and only then, can we begin to appreciate the things He appreciates, love the things He loves and hate the things He hates. His desires become our desires, and we begin to look at life from His perspective. Our maturity in Christ rests on our willingness to abide daily in such a mindset.

Maturity in the Christian life can only be pursued by a believer with a willing and able heart. Such a believer will step around temptations, see beyond failures and endure through trials. He is intrinsically motivated to seek, at all costs, his primary goal: to love God and to know Him *well*.

One of my favorite devotional books in my library is a little book titled, *The Practice of the Presence of God* by

Brother Lawrence. Once a soldier and footman in France in the seventeenth century, Brother Lawrence later became a member of the barefooted Carmelites. His intense love and loyalty toward God impressed an indelible mark on all who came in contact with him.

I'd like to quote a small portion of one of his letters published in this little book. He is writing to a friend, telling him what will be required of him to pursue spiritual maturity in Christ. Take some time to meditate on his words:

> Let all our employment be to *know* God; the more one knows Him, the more one desires to know Him. And as knowledge is commonly the measure of love, the deeper and more extensive our knowledge shall be, the greater will be our love; and if our love of God were great, we should love Him equally in pains and pleasures ... Let us begin to be devoted to Him in good earnest. Let us cast everything besides out of our hearts. He would possess them alone. Beg this favor of Him. If we do what we can on our parts, we shall soon see that change wrought in us which we aspire after.[3]

Do you desire to abide totally in Christ? Do you want to burn on for God despite the surrounding circumstances? Are you willing to live on the Word of God without mixing it with your personal truths? In order for your growth in Christ to move actively onward and in a straight path, these are some of the questions you must be able to say yes to without any hesitation.

In the end, we're going to have to answer for what we did in this life. The words of the apostle Paul remind us that each man's work will some day become evident:

> Each man's work will become evident; for the day will show it, because it is to be revealed with fire; and the fire itself will test the quality of each man's work. If any man's work which he has built upon it

remains, he shall receive a reward. If any man's work is burned up, he shall suffer loss; but he himself shall be saved, yet so as through fire (1 Corinthians 3:13-15).

Are you ready to start making your life count in the kingdom of God? Then let's get going!

For Reflection, Discussion and Action

1. Before you read this chapter, how would you have described *devotion*? Is it any different from how you would describe it now? Name someone you know who displays a devoted character.

2. What things can distract you from your devotion to God?

3. List five things which you do out of your devotion to God. Now ask your spouse (or close friend) to list your five items of devotion without seeing what you've written. Were there differences? If so, why?

4. How often do you pray? Over meals? At church? Before bedtime? How can a recommitment to your devotion to prayer change your current prayer life?

5. Is complete obedience to the truths of God sometimes difficult for you? What kind of personal accountability could you set up that might help you walk in obedience to the truths of God? Write down at least three things which you know you need to commit in obedience to God (perhaps something about your personality, lifestyle or how you treat others).

2

Front-Line Christianity

It is right to be contented with what we have,
but never with what we are.
—Sir James Mackintosh

After fifty-seven miles I had finally caught and passed the second-place rider. Though my legs were beginning to weaken and my body was sending me strong signals to slow down, I pressed on as fast as I could, encouraged by reports that I was only two miles behind the first-place rider.

With about two thousand other participants, I had entered a bicycle ride from Steamboat Springs, Colorado to Vail, Colorado, a distance of more than 100 miles. Though it wasn't officially called a "race," those of us toward the front viewed it as such. Perhaps it was the adolescent competitiveness of our human nature that was showing, because the drama was present and our race was on.

At mile sixty, there was a steep climb of about 1,600 feet in five miles. Having done much of my training in the Rocky Mountains, I figured I could catch the first-place rider by the summit of the climb. As I strained and pushed the pedals, the sweat soaked my shirt. Finally, I came in view of the top of the climb and could see the first-place rider just going over the summit.

I reached the top thirsty and out of breath, but driven by the thought of passing him, I continued to pedal fast down the seven-mile descent. I finally caught him at the bottom of the hill. He was as surprised as I was at our meeting.

Trying to hide my fatigue, I suggested that we ride together the final thirty miles into Vail. He gladly agreed. I took my place behind his rear wheel and together we rode toward the finish line.

After about thirty minutes, he turned and asked if I would take the front. I hesitated. Even though I had been recovering, riding in his draft, I knew it required much more energy to break the wind as the lead rider and I did not have a lot of energy to spare. But I finally agreed.

After taking the front, I began to feel a little guilty for not being willing to break the wind for my new friend before he had to ask. I had comfortably slipped in behind him to save my energy while he worked for me. With this in mind, I decided I would lead out for him the final twenty miles into Vail and give my friend the break he deserved.

What's Holding Us Back?

How much easier it would have been for me to simply go the distance behind another rider! I could have slipped in behind somebody else, followed in his draft all the way to Vail and then had energy to spare.

It seems as though this is a popular practice for Christians. Quite inconspicuously, believers will "ride" in the draft of other believers who are earnestly living their Christianity on the front lines of the battle. Rather than step out and take a firm position when their faith is challenged, these "draft riders" are silent and wait for others to speak out for the faith. If there is a need for someone to lead a Bible study, teach a Sunday school class or simply usher during the worship service, these believers will always balk at offering themselves.

A pastor friend of mine has a truthful little slogan about Christians who are unwilling to take the initiative in any situation: "There are two tragedies in this world. One is being willing and not able, and the other is being able but not willing." It's tragic that some believers apparently consider the price the Lord paid for our sins as not enough to require any sacrifice on their part.

Why would a believer choose to stay comfortably behind the action? I believe there are at least four reasons:

1. Evangelical Rationalism

2. Worldly Compromising

3. Fear

4. Misdirected Priorities

Evangelical Rationalism

To describe "evangelical rationalism," I refer to the church at Ephesus in Revelation 2:

> To the angel of the church in Ephesus write: The One who holds the seven stars in His right hand, the One who walks among the seven golden lampstands, says this:
> "I know your deeds and your toil and perseverance, and that you cannot endure evil men, and you put to the test those who call themselves apostles, and they are not, and you found them to be false; and you have perseverance and have endured for My name's sake and have not grown weary. But I have this

against you, that you have left your first love" (Revelation 2:1-4).

The church at Ephesus was theologically firm and unshakable. They endured through difficulties and were great at spotting phony prophets. So what was the problem? The problem was that their strength was essentially their weakness. As a result of such an outwardly firm and disciplined approach to God, they lost their internal passion and zeal for Him. They emphasized the theological rather than the spiritual.

We easily do the same thing in our churches today when we emphasize form rather than function, position rather than performance and "doing" rather than "being."

Without a passion and zeal for God, we lose our motivation to sacrifice ourselves. God becomes methodical and distant. He is no longer a warm, compassionate and merciful God who desires to draw near to us. He is a Being whose only purpose is to carry out a pre-arranged program, merely using us as His faceless tools.

With such a mindset we will never step out and give of ourselves. After all, how many of us would freely give of our time and energy for someone or something we have no passion for? On the other hand, we would gladly sacrifice for that which we feel intimately close and attached to.

Worldly Compromise

It seems as though it is becoming increasingly fashionable to compromise the truths of God with the changing values of man. For instance, homosexuality was once a condemned practice but is now becoming an accepted alternative lifestyle. The Bible is seen as an archaic system of do's and don'ts with no relevance for today's culture. Consequently, any literal interpretation of God's Word is viewed as absurd and old-fashioned.

Influenced by this world philosophy, spiritually weak believers lack any biblical convictions when push comes to shove. And once a believer has compromised the truths of God, he or she becomes unable or unwilling to take a stand. These Christians assume a low profile in their faith and accept no responsibility for its teaching.

In our battle against worldly compromise, we must never forget nor fail to appropriate that powerful Pauline declaration in Romans 12:2:

> And do not be conformed to this world, but be transformed by the renewing of your mind, that you may prove what the will of God is, that which is good and acceptable and perfect.

Fear

Fear is another reason believers choose not to step out in their faith. To some, fear may be considered more a psychological problem than a spiritual one. But the bottom line is that fear results because our basic understanding of the Word of God is faulty. Without a confident understanding of the Bible's teachings, believers are subject to the debilitating effects of fear.

Often I counsel believers who share with me that they are afraid to pray out loud, attend a Bible study or even join the choir. In my work with them, I frequently discover that the majority of these individuals simply lack a basic knowledge of the Word of God. My prescription? Spend a few months in private study working through handbooks teaching the essentials of the Christian faith.

It is amazing that a few months of disciplined Bible study can do what years of messages from the pulpit cannot. Growing strong in the Christian life requires much more than a weekly visit to a Sunday morning service. It requires a committed, concentrated effort in studying God's Word as well as drawing near to the God of the Word.

Misdirected Priorities

Our fourth factor, misdirected priorities, will certainly prevent us from taking any initiative for the Lord and His work. The major problem here is the fact that we are simply too busy to involve ourselves in anything other than our personal interests. Our attendance at a Sunday morning service is the extent of our spiritual obligation. Any effort to motivate us to give any more of our time will often cause us to retreat and become even more distant to the things of God.

With the onset of the technological age and the electronic media blitz, Christians today are living in the most complex and distracting era of human history. Our lives are being imposed upon by everything from television counseling therapy to automated voice mail. We are daily inundated with competing products all designed to "better" our lives and, of course, our world (not to mention the inventor's pocketbook).

All of this occurs under the erroneous conviction that self-improvement and world harmony are attainable if only we continue to offer improvements for man and his surroundings. Man is at the center of his universe. Humanism has become the philosophy of the time, and any biblical concept which suggests that man is in a fallen state is deemed psychologically destructive and condescending to man's ideals.

With the daily barrage of this calculated persuasion from the television, radio and newspapers, it's no wonder that many Christians struggle with establishing the necessary priorities to help them step forward boldly in their faith.

In Luke 10:38-42, there is an amusing yet powerful story of how our Lord confronted an individual who needed to re-establish her priorities. After a long day's journey, Jesus and His disciples were invited to have dinner and stay the evening at the home of Martha and Mary. During the preparation of the meal, Martha became overwhelmed with the work and was angry that her younger sister, Mary, was not helping her. Mary had chosen instead to sit on the living room floor and listen to Jesus. Martha's outburst of anger and our Lord's response is noteworthy:

> "Lord, do You not care that my sister has left me to do all the serving alone? Then tell her to help me." But the Lord answered and said to her, "Martha, Martha, you are worried and bothered about so many things; but only a few things are necessary, really only one, for Mary has chosen the good part, which shall not be taken away from her" (Luke 10:40b-42).

Our Lord was teaching Martha a very important lesson about her priorities. Though He was not necessarily criticizing Martha for being concerned about the household chores, He was instructing her on what things were *really* important and to set her priorities accordingly. And of the things that are important, really only one is vital and must be our top priority: our acknowledgment and worship of God.

In a day that is becoming increasingly hectic and complex, it is vital that we guard our "good" intentions from preoccupying us with misdirected priorities and outside interests, like Martha had. Such intentions, no matter how "good" we may feel them to be, will only distract our thoughts from the God of our salvation. Our intentions need to be guided by the words that the apostle

Paul sent to the church at Colossae: "Set your mind on the things above, not on the things that are on the earth" (Colossians 3:2).

Moving Up to the Front Lines

What steps can we take to begin the process of moving up to the front lines of our faith? I believe that there are three essential items to begin with. We must be willing to deal with these issues if we are to strengthen our spiritual stand.

First, we must be willing to *let go of our earthly desires.* A close reading of Colossians 3:5-7 reveals that the root of all sin is idolatry (i.e., worshipping anything other than God Himself). In 1 John 2:15,16, the apostle John warns us that if we love the world, the love of God is not in us:

> Do not love the world, nor the things in the world. If anyone loves the world, the love of the Father is not in him. For all that is in the world, the lust of the flesh and the lust of the eyes and the boastful pride of life, is not from the Father, but is from the world.

If we truly intend to step out and take the initiative for God, our heart must not have any other attraction except for God! This concept is absolutely vital to our spiritual growth. Jesus declared in no uncertain terms that "no man can serve two masters; for either he will hate the one and love the other, or he will hold to one and despise the other" (Matthew 6:24).

Our first step to the front line of our faith must be our decided and unconditional willingness to freely let go of every earthly desire which is, or could be, a distraction in our relationship to Jesus Christ.

Second, we must re-affirm our total commitment to *walk faithfully with the Lord despite the costs.*

The Lord requires commitment without reservation. To emphasize that point, Jesus compared it to one of the most important symbols of the Hebrew society—the family.

In Matthew 8:21, one of Jesus' disciples asks Him if he may follow Jesus after his father dies so that he may attend the funeral. Jesus' answer uses paradoxical language: "Follow Me; and allow the [spiritually] dead to bury their own [physically] dead" (Matthew 8:22).

Two chapters later, Jesus again uses the family to illustrate His point: "He who loves father or mother more than Me is not worthy of Me; and he who loves son or daughter more than Me is not worthy of Me" (Matthew 10:37).

To the average Jew in Jesus' day, commitment to one another within the family served as the highest ideal. With this in mind, Jesus compared love and commitment to Him as supreme over the family—mother, father, son and daughter. If we are to follow Christ, He must be our supreme love! We must be totally willing to sacrifice our plans and ambitions if they interfere with God's plans for us.

Here's an illustration. Let's say it's your desire to become a professional ice skater and tour with the Ice Capades. As a young girl, you work very hard for many years. While in college, you try out for the Ice Capades and earn a position. You verbally agree to tour with them for the next five years. But a month before you are to report to training camp, your only surviving parent is paralyzed in a terrible automobile accident.

You are now faced with a difficult decision. Do you place your mother in a convalescent home and head for training camp? Or do you give up your place with the Ice Capades and stay near your mother? The decision will not be an easy one to make. But your deep sense of love and commitment to your mother will direct you by way of your heart to stay with her.

Can you see a similarity to the Christian life? Though our decisions to let go of our distracting earthly desires will not necessarily be easy ones, a deep sense of love and commitment to Jesus Christ will steer us in the right direction. And as we mature spiritually and grow closer to Him, our decisions to forsake those things contrary to our Christian life will become less difficult. Why? Because the Lord's desires become your desires as you learn to see life from His perspective: "Delight yourself in the LORD; and He will give you the desires of your heart" (Psalm 37:4).

Once we have freely let go of all distracting earthly desires and have reaffirmed our commitment to Christ, our final step is to *embrace a Christ-like servant attitude.*

In observing the life of Christ, it is not difficult to recognize the servant-like character of our Lord. He said Himself that He did not come to be served, but to serve (Matthew 20:28). Perhaps His most humble example of servanthood was when He washed the feet of the disciples. Here was the creator of the universe stooping to wash the dirty feet of men! Yet He served without question and instructed the disciples that they must learn to do the same (John 13:14).

Being a servant is much more than offering our time here and there. Servanthood is not evident in what we *do*, but in what we *are*. Servanthood is an attitude of the heart which displays itself through a gentle, humble and respectful character. Perhaps Tryon Edwards said it best: "True humility is not an abject, groveling, self-despising spirit: It is but a right estimate of ourselves as God sees us."[1]

Developing a servant's heart will not be too difficult if the first two steps are earnestly pursued. Perhaps you'll find your difficulty will be just wanting to begin step one. But if your desire is to truly serve God on the front lines of the battle, your decision has been made: You must rid yourself of everything that may prevent you from becoming single-minded. And as Paul reminded young Timothy, "No soldier in active service entangles himself in the affairs of everyday life" (2 Timothy 2:4a).

For Reflection, Discussion and Action

1. In what ways have you been "holding back" in your faith? What has been causing you to hold back?

2. Four reasons for holding back were mentioned in this chapter. Which can you relate to the most? Why?

3. List some things in your life you can relate to from the story of Mary and Martha in Luke 10:38-42. Are you more like Mary or Martha?

4. Write down as many earthly desires that you have which could possibly serve as distractions to your spiritual life. Which one will be the most difficult to let go of? Why?

5. What does it mean to "count the costs" in our walk with the Lord? In what ways have you had to count the cost in your own life?

6. How would you describe someone who exhibits a true servant's heart?

3

Laying Out the Game Plan

Where there is no vision, the people perish
(Proverbs 29:18, KJV).

I recently read an amusing story about a pilot who was flying his light plane low over Devil's Creek in Alaska. To his surprise, he saw a black bear walking aimlessly in circles with a large can stuck over its head. Apparently the bear had been rummaging through some garbage for food and had pushed its head into the can and could not pull it out. A rescue party was flown in to tranquilize the bear and remove the can. By the five smooth and worn circular paths in the thick blanket of leaves, the rescue party estimated that the bear had walked perhaps close to 500 miles in circles before being freed.

After reading that story, I started to think about the many different paths my own life has taken since meeting Christ in 1972. Some paths were aimless and merely intended to kill time. Some were fairly consistent with my goals. And some were clearly a result of my spiritual ambition and desire to please the Lord. But no matter what path I've taken, I know that the Lord has been with me and has allowed me to learn from both the good and the bad along the way.

If you were to chart out the next thirty years of your life, what would you do? Where would you go? What would you like to become? And what place would God have in your priorities?

After graduating from high school I remember thinking that I would just continue in the building trade with my father. After all, I enjoyed the work and made pretty good money. Since I hadn't done very well in school, I didn't really care about college. But when most of my friends decided to attend at least a junior college, I thought, *Why not?* It couldn't hurt as long as I didn't take any English courses—I had flunked out of English my senior year in high school. So my thirty-year plan after high school was to work in the construction trade and take a few college courses here and there.

Little did I know that just a short while after high school I would be challenged with the truths of God and later trust my life to Him. At that moment, my whole life and my original plans were turned upside down. As I refocused my sights to know God better, I decided to complete my college education. My new plan was to trust God and submit to His complete leading in my life. To this day, I am anxious and excited about what's next for me on God's agenda.

It disturbs me when I see believers who basically choose not to experience growth in Christ. They walk aimlessly through the routine of life, always in motion but showing no progress. They contribute little toward the advancement of the cause of Christ. When God does something special in their life, they probably will not even notice it. Their interests lie only in what is tangible.

As Christians, I believe we should be anxious about what lies ahead as well as excited about what God is doing in our lives at present. To enjoy God's plan to its fullest, we need to design a biblical strategy for living and establish spiritual goals for the future.

A Strategy for Living in Christ

In this section, my objective is not to present a "fast-food" type strategy for spiritual growth. Such a plan would be too easy to latch onto without much consideration. Rather, I'm going to provide the resource information. Hopefully, you will be motivated and strengthened in the direction God is taking you. I believe the Holy Spirit is uniquely at work in each of us and a strategy for one may be different from another.

To begin with, allow me first to define what I mean by "strategy." "Strategy" does not imply *how* we should live in Christ. How we should live is clearly laid out for us throughout Scripture. Rather, "strategy" emphasizes a *plan* to help us within our unique and specific strengths to accomplish the things that we know God wants us to do.

For example, let's say a football team has a great running back and a weak passing quarterback on its roster. In an upcoming game, they will be playing a team whose quarterback is one of the best passing quarterbacks in the league. For this game, our football team establishes a game plan to work at maintaining possession of the ball twice as long as the other team. In order to do that, their plan is to run the ball as frequently as possible, utilizing their talented running back.

You'll notice that their game plan does not include the fundamentals of *how* to play football. It is assumed that each player understands the importance of blocking, tackling and scoring. But the game plan is established based on the strengths and weaknesses of our football team in order to help it reach its ultimate goal of victory.

Our spiritual "game plan" uses the same principles. Depending on what spiritual gifts and talents God has endowed us with, we should establish a personal plan that will help us live out the spiritual truths He has already established for our growth. The ultimate victory occurs when Christ comes to meet His own in the last days.

I've adopted a strategy which has been the basis for all my plans: Live the Christian life as though Christ is coming back tomorrow and plan as though He is coming back in a hundred years.

In my life, living by example is a big part of my Christian plan. To display a Christ-like character is an essential ingredient to my testimony. As a teacher, leader and parent, I have a great opportunity to teach as much through what I *do* as what I *say* from the lectern, pulpit and dinner table. And as I grasp the truths of God through appropriating His Word in my life, I can evangelize and disciple people both by my example and my words.

If I were to diagram this strategy, it might look something like this:

The point at which my Christian testimony will pierce into a lost world

My plan to display Christ in my life

By my living example

By my spoken and written words

My strategy to live out the truths of God

To live as though Christ is returning tomorrow, but plan as though He is coming back in a hundred years

How I learn to live the Christian life (appropriation)

Accountability
Godly counsel
The Word of God

The bottom third of the triangle represents the sources from which I learn and appropriate the truths of God into my life: 1. the Word of God; 2. the counsel of godly men and women; and 3. the wisdom developed and nurtured through my accountability to the individuals whom God has placed me in submission to.

The middle of the triangle represents my *strategy* to undertake my plan.

The upper third of the triangle represents my *plan* to display the truths of God in my life before a lost world. I execute this plan using two distinct means: my everyday example of living out the truths of God and my preaching, teaching and writing. Note that the left area is a little larger, reflecting my planned emphasis on being an example.

All three levels build to a point in my life which will pierce the world and carry on the Great Commission of evangelism and discipleship. This entire process is never at rest. It is always moving upward, being continually generated by new discoveries and revelations which come to light in my life through the Word of God and godly counsel.

My personal strategy for living my life in Christ is based on the conviction that my spiritual gifts lie in the area of exhortation and teaching. Your gifts will most likely be different.[1] For the sake of an example, let's say that your gifts are in the areas of evangelism and teaching. Using my diagram to develop your plan, you would probably place a greater emphasis on your spoken and written word, rather than your example. If your gifts lie in the areas of helps and service, you may develop a strategy that emphasizes your example almost completely, with very little emphasis on your spoken or written word.

In terms of strategy development, there are many

other ways to execute your plan besides the two I have listed. For example, you might want to consider the ministry of music, servanthood, friendship, prayer, organizer/planner. With your personal spiritual evaluation and a little creativity, the list could be endless.

If your Christian life seems aimless, you need to get busy and develop a strategy for working with the special skills, gifts and talents God has graciously given you. Do not be a believer who merely walks in circles like our bear did. Rather, move out and press on for the glory of God. Consider these words of the apostle Paul:

> I press on toward the goal for the prize of the upward call of God in Christ Jesus (Philippians 3:14).

> Do you not know that those who run in a race all run, but only one receives the prize? Run in such a way that you may win . . . Therefore I run in such a way as not without *aim* (1 Corinthians 9:24,26b, italics mine).

Establishing Spiritual Goals

Once we have established our strategy, we need to ask ourselves what we want to accomplish as we go. Most likely we will not accomplish very much if we don't set some goals.

It would be aimless to jump in our car and develop a strategy for driving it (which might be to drive in the right lane at 55 m.p.h. with stops every three hours) without a destination. Likewise, drawing up a strategy for living the Christian life will not take us very far if we don't know what we want or need to accomplish along the way.

I believe that developing our strategy should precede our goal setting simply because our strategy will help to define our capabilities and our limits. This, in turn, causes us to create more realistic and measurable goals.

Goal-setting is a challenge, though, simply because we know that once we've set goals, we will have to work to complete them. As a young man in high school, I hated to set academic goals. I wanted the freedom to be lazy. I didn't want the pressure of failing and letting myself and my parents down. Needless to say, I did not accomplish anything academically significant during those years.

But not surprisingly, when it came to athletics— more specifically football and weight training—I did not mind setting goals. I wanted to be first string on the football team and I needed a strong and impressive physique to get there.

Isn't that just like human nature? Won't we strive only for what our heart is truly set on? To insure that we accomplish the goals we set, we must have a heart for God and a willingness to be committed totally to His ways: "For where your treasure is, there will your heart be also" (Matthew 6:21). If this is the case in your life, then we're ready to proceed.

The Goal-Setting Process

First, set a time limit to accomplish your goals within one year. A longer time may cause you to become impatient or distracted, and you'll subtly lose sight of your original goals.

Second, give a copy of your goals to a friend, spouse or parent for accountability purposes. Let them know what you desire to accomplish.

And last, make sure that the goals you set are reachable and measurable. For example, let's say you set a goal to lead 500 people to Christ in the coming year. Well, unless you are Billy Graham, such a goal is most likely unreachable. Perhaps a goal of five or ten people may be more realistic.

In terms of being measurable, a goal should not have an abstract result. For example, the goal, "I will grow deeper in the knowledge of my faith through the next year," has no tangible way to show it's been accomplished. A more measurable way to write this goal would be: "I will grow deeper in the knowledge of my faith through the next year by completing a devotional guide and memorizing fifty Bible verses." Now the goal has two measurable items to help determine if you did, indeed, grow deeper in the knowledge of your faith.

Keep these things in mind as you think through your goals. Let's get started:

Step 1: Set Two or Three Goals

First, ask yourself two questions:

1. What would I *like* to do spiritually through the next year?

2. What do I *need* to do spiritually through the next year?

There may be a whole host of things you want to do. Would you like to read through the Bible? Begin a prayer diary? Memorize Scripture? Lead a certain person or persons to Christ? Serve on a short-term mission?

Write them all down on a piece of paper and then, after spending some time in prayer, choose the top two or three which are the most reachable and measurable. Write them here:

Goal 1:

Goal 2:

Goal 3:

Step 2: List the Steps Necessary to Accomplish Each Goal

In this step you will write down what you need to do to accomplish each goal you have listed. For example, if your first goal is to lead "John" to Christ, what things can you do to help accomplish this? Pray for him—how and when? Spend time with him? Invite him to a Bible study? Share the gospel with him? Write down the steps you can take to help reach each of the goals you have listed.

Steps for Goal 1:

Steps for Goal 2:

Steps for Goal 3:

Step 3: Prioritize Your Goals

Now it's time to prioritize your goals. Before you do this, however, spend some time alone with the Lord in prayer seeking His wisdom and guidance. You do not want to strive for goals that may not be useful to His kingdom or that are more of a product of your fleshly desires than His holy will. Seek the counsel of others as well before you complete this step.

After you've prayerfully gone through your goals, prioritize them below:

Goal A:

Goal B:

Goal C:

The Final Step: Set a Time Frame for Your First Steps

In this final step, set the gears in motion by setting a deadline to complete the very first step you have listed to reach each goal. Make your deadlines realistic, but keep them challenging:

First Step Deadline Date for Goal A: _____

First Step Deadline Date for Goal B: _____

First Step Deadline Date for Goal C: _____

When you've met the deadlines for your first steps, go back and set deadlines for the rest of your steps.

I believe if you have set some measurable and reachable goals by following the steps listed, you are well on your way to becoming more spiritually productive for the Lord. You not only have a strategy, but now you also have a purpose—a tangible reflection of your faith.

Be careful, though, not to assume that developing a strategy and setting goals will create instant spiritual maturity or discipline. They're important, but they're only a part of the whole picture. We must never forget that within our relationship with Christ there must be a sincere measure of intangible faith:

> And without faith it is impossible to please Him, for he who comes to God must believe that He is, and that He is a rewarder of those who seek Him (Hebrews 11:6).

For Reflection, Discussion and Action

1. What, if any, was your strategy for living the Christian life before you read this chapter? What was your plan to carry out your strategy?

2. Complete the steps for goal-setting and share your goals with a friend.

3. While goal-setting is an important part of the spiritual growth process, without faith we get nowhere. Describe the role faith plays in your Christian life. What aspects of your relationship with Christ depend on a "sincere measure of intangible faith"?

4

Firming Up
Our Foundation

How blessed is the man whose strength is in Thee
(Psalm 84:5).

In high school, one of my favorite sports was football. Though I was not very big, I went out for the school
team in my junior and senior years. I tried my best and
worked hard in practice, so occasionally I was rewarded
with some actual playing time.

To me, though, one of the most interesting times of
the game was not during the game itself, but before the
game. Each team would take half the field and do their
warm-ups. During the calisthenics and play rehearsals,
each of us would take turns looking across the field in
order to size up the other team. How many big players
did they have? What did their quarterback look like?
Who had the better looking jerseys?

This pre-game psyche usually reached its climax at
the center of the field during the toss of the coin. Each
team captain would approach the other with his chest out
and a "Clint Eastwood" expression painted on. And
when it came time to shake hands, we always tried to

squeeze the other guys' hands as hard as we could to let them know in advance that we were strong.

The pre-game power play is probably most evident at the start of a boxing match—and in some ways it is rather amusing. The two boxers meet at the center of the ring to receive their instructions and shake hands, but rarely do you see boxers actually listening to what the referee is saying. Instead, they are staring down each other, attempting to non-verbally communicate their power and toughness and hoping to mentally gain an edge over their opponent.

Sometimes I think believers take the same approach in their battle with Satan, the flesh and the world. They try to "stare down" a greedy opportunity or a lustful temptation by announcing that it could never happen to them or refusing to recognize a problem may exist.

Such an approach is destined to fail. God never intended nor prepared man to fight the battle alone. He intended man to take up the armor of God (Ephesians 6:11-18) and be on guard (1 Peter 5:8) lest he should fall. Yet immature and prideful believers continue to try and face the Adversary alone and soon fall to temptation or gross sin.

It is imperative for Christians to know and understand what they are up against. Among other things, Satan can disguise himself as an "angel of light" (2 Corinthians 11:14) and has blinded the minds of the unbelieving (2 Corinthians 4:4).

I can certainly appreciate Paul's concern for the church at Corinth. By the time he had written 2 Corinthians, he had already written three other letters (two are now lost) to the church. He was troubled by their vulnerability to be misled by false prophets. Toward the end of the last letter to the church, Paul writes:

But I am afraid, lest as the serpent deceived Eve
by his craftiness, your minds should be led astray from
the simplicity and purity of devotion to Christ (2
Corinthians 11:3).

Rather than try to stare down the Adversary, I think
there is a far more biblical and realistic approach to
knowing and understanding who and what our foes are.
I refer to this approach as the "J. Edgar Hoover Principle."

During the fifties and early sixties, Hoover as-
sembled teams of FBI agents to confiscate counterfeit
money. In order to teach his agents how to recognize
phony bills, he would have them spend several days
doing nothing more than handling real money. Through
this training the agents learned, beyond any measure of
doubt, what the real bills looked and felt like. When a
phony bill came along, Hoover's agents could spot it
immediately.

Scripture teaches that we are to learn to accurately
handle the Word of God (2 Timothy 2:15) so that we will
not be misled by false teachers (2 Timothy 2:17,18). By
knowing the Word of God well, we'll be able to spot the
phonies in an instant!

But regardless of how close we feel to our God, we
must be on guard. We may become so confident in our
position in Christ that we subtly drift from our dependence on Him and become self-contained and inde-
pendent. Nothing would please Satan more. Satan claims
a great victory in the fall of a believer whose "close" walk
with the Lord is well known and respected.

All Show and No Grow

Through most of my high school and college days,
I worked for a man whose business was remodeling

homes. It was grimy and often dangerous work, but it paid well and I learned a lot about building in the process.

One of the tasks I enjoyed least was digging dirt. To me, there was nothing more humbling than to dig in a trench all day long. Jobs that called for an added room above an existing room or garage meant several days of digging by shovel for everyone on the crew.

With such a job, the city building codes required us to dig a trench a foot wide and three feet deep alongside the existing foundation. We would then pour concrete in this trench to firm up the existing foundation so it could support the weight created by the additional room.

My trench-digging days illustrate an important aspect of the Christian life. Let's say at the start of your Christian walk your life is like a single-floor room. As you grow and mature in the Lord, you decide to step out and pursue a deep love relationship with God.[1] We'll call this the process of adding an additional room above your existing single-floor room.

A deeper relationship will require greater responsibility as well as greater personal cost. It will cost you more of your time and energy, and in some ways it may cost you financially. It will most likely introduce you to new undertakings such as teaching a Bible study or even preaching in a church service. Your leadership by example will come into greater scrutiny, not to mention that as a teacher you will be subject to a stricter judgment by the Lord (James 3:1).

With this increased responsibility will come the added pressure to maintain your close walk with God before men. But if you have not prepared or strengthened your spiritual foundation, you could very well fall as fast as you rose in your deeper walk with Christ.

When a believer in this situation falls to sin, many

times he does so as a result of his own pride. He did not take the right steps in strengthening his foundation and, consequently, developed a false sense of confidence—a confidence founded only in the flesh.

In such a confidence, our first response to temptation will often be to "stare down" the sin like two boxers. But we are destined to fail. Satan is not an adversary we can handle ourselves—never! We can face him off only from behind the cross of Christ.

You do not have to look very far in the Scriptures to read about individuals who were close with the Lord but, for one reason or another, succumbed to sin: Adam and Eve, Moses, Job, Saul, David, Peter—just to mention a few. If you study the lives of these individuals, you will find that often the lack of a deeper, more rooted foundation contributed to their fall. Let's take a look at the apostle Peter.

Peter was a man full of confidence in his early walk with the Lord. He would often speak out for his faith and boldly declare that he would never fall away (Mark 14:29). He even seemed to grow closer to Christ as His arrest and crucifixion neared (Matthew 26:34,35). Yet despite all his bold statements, Peter denied our Lord three times before a young servant girl. He crumbled in the face of pressure.

What happened to our hero? Why did he, in the midst of perhaps his greatest time of strength and boldness for Christ, fall to sin by cowardly denying the Lord? I believe he fell because he had not developed a deep foundation for his faith to grow unshakably strong. Peter was more "show" than strength. He had a big profession but poor performance.

Before we come down too hard on Peter, though, we need to mention the rest of his story. Some thirty years later, through the inspiration of the Holy Spirit, Peter wrote 1 and 2 Peter. In those two books, we see a different Peter. He is no longer the cowardly man we spoke of earlier. Now he is a mature and sincere man who is steadfast in his faith. His letters encouraged Jewish Christians scattered throughout Asia Minor who were suffering under the terrible scourges of the Neronian persecutions—one of the ten great persecutions of the early church.

You see, something happened to Peter which caused him to deepen his foundation of faith and love in Jesus Christ. Despite the persecution he was facing under Nero (which was far greater than the challenge from the servant girl some thirty years earlier), he continued in his faith without wavering.

One of the most important reasons for strengthening our spiritual foundation is to better prepare ourselves to handle the persecution from the world. Paul reminded young Timothy that "all who desire to live godly lives in Christ Jesus will be persecuted" (2 Timothy 3:12). Just as our second-story room needs to have a much larger foundation to support the added weight, so must our foundation of faith and love in Jesus Christ increase if we choose to become more spiritually visible and accountable.

But do not lose heart when the going gets rough. Peter encourages that we will be blessed if we choose to suffer for Christ:

> If you are reviled for the name of Christ, you are blessed, because the Spirit of glory and of God rests upon you (1 Peter 4:14).

> And after you have suffered for a little while, the God of all grace, who called you to His eternal glory in Christ, will Himself perfect, confirm, strengthen and establish you (1 Peter 5:10).

So what happened to Peter that encouraged his foundation of love and faith in Christ to grow? What caused him to change from the big-shot, "all talk and no action" guy to the wise and humble servant of God? Well, I believe there were two key areas within his character that were drastically affected as he matured in Christ:

1. *Submission*. Peter finally understood the principle of "dying to self" while living daily for Christ.

2. *Holiness*. Peter realized the importance of confirming his faith through godly living.

Let's take a brief look at both of these areas.

Adopting the "Gethsemane Mindset"

In looking back at Peter in the Gospels, it's not too difficult to see that he had a terrible time with submitting and putting the needs of others first. Even though Peter was usually the first of all the disciples to step up and "defend" the Lord, it would appear he did not do it as much out of a sheer love for Christ as for his own pride and position before the other apostles.

For example, consider the story of Jesus walking on the water to the disciples (Matthew 14). You might recall that as Jesus neared the disciples' boat, they thought He was a ghost and were afraid. But Peter, wanting to display his courage, boldly declared, "Lord, if it is You, command me to come to You on the water" (Matthew 14:28). Well, you know the story. Peter started walking on the water toward Jesus but soon became afraid and began to sink. Without hesitation, Jesus grabbed his hand and pulled him up.

If I had been one of the disciples observing all this, I probably would have broken out in laughter once Peter was on board. After all, this wouldn't have been the first time I had witnessed Peter getting into trouble because of his egocentric ways.

But even though Peter later failed his Lord in an hour of crisis, he was restored and recommissioned by Jesus after the resurrection. And in the book of Acts, beginning with his great sermon in chapter 2, we see Peter becoming a man of conviction—not the impulsive, presumptuous individual we had seen in the past (Matthew 14:28; 16:22; 17:4). Now Peter was the respected leader and spokesman of the twelve, and eventually he was used of God to bring salvation to the Jews.

Only a man who is willing to give up the rights to his own life can ever make such a change. Peter finally understood what Jesus meant when He prayed, "My Father, if it is possible, let this cup pass from Me; yet not as I will, but as Thou wilt" (Matthew 26:39). Jesus had said *no* to His own will and *yes* to His Father's will. Peter learned to submit to God's will for him and not demand his own will for his life.

Vernon Grounds, in his powerful book *Radical Commitment*, refers to this idea of death to self as the "Gethsemane mindset." He writes that this mindset was demonstrated by Jesus when He prayed in the Garden of Gethsemane, "Not my will, Father, but your will be done."[2] He clearly defines how we can develop the "Gethsemane mindset":

> It is a renunciation of our own very human feelings, desires, hopes, dreams, and ambitions in order that the purposes of God may be accomplished. We develop this mindset as we follow the example of Jesus. We set our minds on doing the will of God, obeying Him even though obedience involves self-denial, the surrender of anything that would interfere with the fulfillment of the divine purpose. We do this in the confidence that, as we follow our Lord's ex-

ample, we are going to experience beyond loss and loneliness and the pain, the joy and blessing and glory which mean unimaginable self-fulfillment.[3]

Self-denial for the purpose of accomplishing the will of God is a mark of spiritual maturity. Learning self-denial is a major step in strengthening our foundation.

Are you willing to put to death your desires, hopes and dreams if they are not in accord with God's purposes? Are you willing to forsake your selfishness and conceit in order to humbly submit to God's authority over your plans? If so, you're beginning to dig your trench a little deeper.

An Emphasis in Godly Living

The second area I believe vital in strengthening our foundation in Christ is personal holiness. Peter wrote that the people of God are called to be holy:

> Obey God because you are His children; don't slip back into your old ways—doing evil because you knew no better. But be holy now in everything you do, just as the Lord is holy, who invited you to be His child. He Himself has said, "You must be holy, for I am holy" (1 Peter 1:14-16, TLB).

In this passage, Peter reminds us that even though we know Christ, we can still feel the pull back to our old sinful ways. We must strengthen our foundation by living a holy life. This will help to separate us from the temptations and deceptions of our old sinful nature.

Defining holiness is difficult and sometimes controversial. There are a great variety of definitions, depending on one's particular theological persuasion. For our purposes, I prefer to keep the definition as biblically concise and to the point as we can without compromising any of its power.

Very simply, holiness is our devotion to and reflection of a holy God who is, among other things, merciful, just, loving and pure. We are to be set apart—not merely for the sake of being different, but as a result of the qualities of God penetrating through our life in everything we do. It must be added that this is done by yielding to the control of the Holy Spirit.

Let me illustrate. As a young Christian, there was a man in my church whom I greatly admired. He was honest, sincere, caring, patient and loving. He was the finest example of a Christian I had ever met. I admired him so much that soon I found myself wanting to walk like him and talk like him. I wanted to imitate everything about his life.

Finally, I went to him one day and asked if I could spend an hour or two with him to ask him some questions I had about God. What I was really wanting to learn was how he lived his life for God the way he did.

Toward the end of our conversation, I asked him if I could be accountable to him because I wanted to grow in my faith. He replied by challenging me with these questions: "Are you willing to submit yourself to suggestions, admonitions and criticisms for your life? Are you willing to make changes when changes are needed?" His questions hit me like a ton of bricks. I knew accountability meant commitment, but not necessarily opening up my entire life to his scrutiny. It scared me, so I told him I would get back to him in a few days.

That night, I read through 1 Peter. To say the least, I was convicted by such powerful statements as: "gird up your minds for action" (1 Peter 1:13); proclaim "the excellencies of Him who has called you" (1 Peter 2:9);

"submit yourselves for the Lord's sake" (1 Peter 2:13, 18); and "sanctify Christ as Lord in your hearts" (1 Peter 3:15).

The whole idea of confirming my faith in Christ through my thoughts and actions finally got through to me. Holiness was not something to perform, but something to be! Placing myself in submission to be accountable to my friend was part of my willingness to live my life as a reflection of God's holiness. You see, if we truly desire to deepen our foundation of faith in Christ, we must live like Christ. We must be like Christ.

For young or immature believers, this seems to be one of the most difficult barriers to cross when choosing to grow deeper in the Christian life. New believers want to cling to much of their past life with its earthly desires and values. They are not sure if they want to adopt the holiness of Christ totally in their lives. Why? Because embracing His holiness may demand that they change. They may have to make adjustments in their language, or their eating and drinking habits, or the way they talk about people. This is why our first step toward developing a deeper, firmer foundation for Christ must be our willingness to deny ourself for the purposes of God. Then, and only then, will we be able to embrace the holiness of God in such a way that anything outside of His holiness would be insulting not only to God, but to us as well.

In our choice to grow deeper in our relationship with God, we must be careful not to face the Adversary in our own power along the way. Our job is to firm up our foundation to fight the battle in Christ's power by becoming like Him. So let us put to death our selfishness and pursue His holiness. Then we'll be able to say along with the apostle Paul:

> I count all things to be loss in view of the surpassing value of knowing Christ Jesus my Lord, for whom

I have suffered the loss of all things, and count them but rubbish in order that I may gain Christ . . . Brethren, I do not regard myself as having laid hold of it yet; but one thing I do: forgetting what lies behind and reaching forward to what lies ahead (Philippians 3:8,13).

For Reflection, Discussion and Action

1. What is your usual first response to temptation? Describe your last battle with sin. How did you fight? What was the outcome?

2. Have you ever become so confident about something that you dropped your guard and were soon overcome by the very thing you thought could never harm you? Explain.

3. Before reading this chapter, what steps had you taken to firm up your spiritual foundation? What will you do differently now?

4. Consider the two concepts of submission and holiness. Which is the most difficult for you to pursue? Why?

5. Name some things in your life that you did not want to "give up" at the time of conversion, but have since let go of. How has God blessed you for your obedience?

6. What do you need to do now in your pursuit of the holiness of God?

Preparing to See the Finish

Looking for the blessed hope and the appearing of the glory of our great God and Savior, Jesus Christ (Titus 2:13).

A new Christian once asked A. W. Tozer, "What does it mean to be crucified with Christ?"

Dr. Tozer replied, "To be crucified with Christ means three things. First, the man on the cross faces in only one direction: 'I press on toward the goal for the prize of the upward call of God in Christ Jesus' (Philippians 3:14).

"Second, it means not going back: 'But My righteous one shall live by faith; and if he shrinks back, My soul has no pleasure in him' (Hebrews 10:38).

"Third, it means ceasing to have personal plans and living only to bring glory to Christ: 'But rise, and enter the city, and it shall be told you what you must do (Acts 9:6); 'Christ shall even now, as always, be exalted in my body, whether by life or by death' (Philippians 1:20b)."

Dr. Tozer was speaking not just about a commitment to Christ, but a *lifetime* of commitment to Christ.

There is a difference. Once a person trusts his life to Christ, he is committing himself to a lifetime of service and obedience to God. It is not a short-term agreement requiring only temporary changes and responsibilities. Nor is it a transitory relationship merely designed to douse personal "grass fires." Rather, it is an eternal relationship intended to bring glory to God and mercy, peace, contentment and love to the believer.

But often I watch new "believers" treat their walk in Christ as a sort of temporary deliverance or passing fad. They seem to say and do all the right things, but often in a burst of energy. Over a period of years or even months, their interests drift. Faithful church attendance drops down to occasional visits. If confronted, these folks will insist that everything's fine with their life—there is no need to be worried about them.

I have watched this happen many times to young people. A young man or woman will be facing a difficult decision or crisis. In the midst of it, these kids will open up to the gospel. But once their situation is resolved and everything is back to normal, their interest in the things of God fades. Commitment to Christ was merely a temporary refuge. Perhaps their confession of faith in Christ was not a heart-felt one but a last-ditch effort motivated by fear.

The principles we have looked at in the preceding chapters (setting goals, firming up our foundation, dying to self) are indeed excellent guidelines for us if we intend to grow deeper in our walk with Christ. But what we must realize is that these principles are meant to be approached from a long-term perspective. Setting goals should not be a one-shot effort but a yearly challenge. Dying to self is not a principle we learn overnight. It is a mental attitude which we will have to work at for the rest of our lives—thanks to our sin nature. And need I mention that the act of submission will not just automatically occur? Growing deep in Christ is a daily and permanent practice that will require our time, effort and energy until He takes us home. It cannot be achieved through a sudden, temporary burst of energy.

I still vividly recall being told as a new Christian that the Christian life is like riding a bicycle: Once you learn it, you will never forget. Nothing could be farther from the truth! While it is true that a believer is eternally saved, living the Christian life is a day-by-day, month-by-month, year-by-year process. In this process the Lord leads us through many different situations and trials with the intent of perfecting us to His glory (Romans 5:3-11; Philippians 1:6; Colossians 1:27,28). God never intended for us to simply arrive at our new position in Christ and remain there.

It is easy to understand why some new believers fail to comprehend the idea of a long-term commitment to Christ. In our day, the value of long-term commitment to anything is losing its honor. Marriage, the one institution which carries the vow of lifetime commitment, is no longer viewed by the majority as such. It is now seen as a contract between two people and, regardless of the formality, contracts can be broken.

We are living in a world where values change. We are told that change is inherent within progress, and progress is viewed as the food of a productive life. Therefore, our lifestyle, our goals, our values, our vocation and even our religion will be encouraged to change in order to remain in the progressive mainstream of our society. Consequently, our belief system, which once viewed our conversion to Christ as our finest decision, may change until we no longer believe that Christ must be our number-one priority and our ultimate authority.

Conforming to This World

The apostle Peter admonishes us to be obedient children of God and "not be conformed to the former lusts which were yours in your ignorance" (1 Peter 1:14). "Not be conformed to our former lusts" simply means for us to keep ourselves from our previous lifestyle which patterned itself after the behavior and customs of the world.

I am sure that most of us did some things in our youth that later in life we looked back on with embarrassment. I remember in ninth grade, during the 1968 presidential elections, my buddies and I got hold of more than a thousand bumper stickers which read, "Nixon For President" and "Humphrey in '68." On several successive nights during the week before the elections, my friends and I went out and put these stickers on everything from street signs to house windows. On each of the following mornings, we would see all the stickers and just laugh!

The problem with these stickers, though, was that they did not come off very easily. For the next several years, the remains of some of these stickers were still visible. As I got older, I felt more foolish every time I saw them.

Finally, I could not stand it any longer. A few months after I became a Christian, I decided to clean off every sticker that still remained. One in particular was now firmly ingrained into a cedar fence. This cedar fence was owned by a man whom I did not care for much. To put my conscience at ease, though, I knew I had no choice but to go to Tom, apologize and ask if I could work at removing the remains of the sticker on his fence.

My confession was received with a suspicious stare, but Tom finally agreed to let me remove the sticker so long as I did not ruin his fence. It turned out that the sticker could not be taken off without ruining the board it was stuck to. I had to replace and paint some of the fence which ended up costing me about $50.

But regardless of the cost, once the fence was repaired, I felt so much better. My foolishness during that week in ninth grade no longer haunted me. And I also had a new-found relationship with ol' Tom.

Two of the guys who had originally helped me paste those stickers heard that I went back and cleaned them up. Not suprisingly, they kidded me about becoming a "do-gooder" and not wanting to do any more "crazy" things or have any more "fun." Though their kidding hurt in some ways, my heart was still at ease. My new life in Christ now meant more than the world to me.

I think this is what Peter had in mind when he wrote that we must not be conformed to our former lusts. In our ignorance, we behaved according to our personal desires. In other words, it is impossible for the non-believer to understand and appropriate the truths of God. And now that I am a Christian, I must not confuse what I once considered okay in my ignorance (before Christ) with my understanding now in Christ. If I had decided as a believer to go back with my friends and do some "crazy" things, I would be a disobedient child.

I believe this is often what happens to a believer who drifts from his relationship with God within just a few months or years of his conversion. After exhibiting a burst of energy in his new life for Christ, he still finds himself very attracted to the things of the world and is unwilling to completely let go of his previous worldly lifestyle. Though he may faithfully attend church and a Bible study, his abusive language and deceitful tongue are still uncontrolled when he's not with other Christians. He is, in a sense, leading a double life.

Taking the "Island" by Storm

A true lifetime commitment to Christ requires our sanctification in Christ. Within evangelical circles, it is generally agreed that sanctification simply means to be set apart for God's purposes. But I believe there are two very important aspects to sanctification which must be clearly understood. The first is *positional* sanctification. In 1 Corinthians 6:9-11 we read:

> Or do you not know that the unrighteous shall not inherit the kingdom of God? Do not be deceived; neither fornicators, nor idolaters, nor adulterers, nor effeminate, nor homosexuals, nor thieves, nor the covetous, nor drunkards, nor revilers, nor swindlers, shall inherit the kingdom of God. And such were some of you; but you were washed, but you were sanctified, but you were justified in the name of the Lord Jesus Christ, and in the Spirit of our God.

In this passage, Paul reminds the Christians at Corinth of their former devilish ways. He then points out that as a result of their new life in Christ, they *were* sanctified (i.e., set apart) unto God. This sanctifying grace, which took place at conversion, separated them in the eyes of God from their former worldly practices and made them saints in the family of God.

This concept is later affirmed in Hebrews 10:10 where the writer reminds us that as a result of Christ doing the will of God in becoming the sacrifice for sin, "we have been sanctified through the offering of the body of Jesus Christ once for all."

The second aspect to sanctification is *progressive* sanctification: By an act of his own will, a believer sets himself apart to God so that he is controlled by the Holy Spirit. In Romans 12:1 we read:

> I urge you therefore, brethren, by the mercies of

God, to present your bodies a living and holy sacrifice, acceptable to God, which is your spiritual service of worship.

The verb translated "to present" in this passage can also mean "to set oneself apart unto God."[1] Paul is urging us to set ourselves apart to God by an act of our own will. This is different from God setting us apart. In our position before God, we *were* sanctified by Him (positional sanctification). In our daily life, we *are being* sanctified as we yield control to the Holy Spirit to mature us in His grace and knowledge (progressive sanctification).

Several years ago I read an interesting illustration which helped me understand positional and progressive sanctification. It was in a book titled, *How Come It's Taking Me So Long To Get Better?* by Lane Adams. Adams was a military man who had served with the Pacific fleet in World War II. He developed his illustration from his military experience.

The U.S. Marines confronted the Japanese on hundreds of different islands scattered throughout the South Pacific during World War II. Adams described how the Marines would select an island for invasion. Once the decision was made and a strategic section of the island was targeted, the Marines would storm the island in amphibious vehicles and establish a "beachhead." When this was done, they would radio back to their convoy ships, "The Marines have landed. The situation is well in control." From this beachhead, the Marines would very deliberately and precisely move into the island, purging out the enemy until the entire island was swept clean. This operation sometimes took days and sometimes months, but the Marines always pushed forward to victory.

It might seem a bit unusual for the Marines to radio back to their fleet that the situation was "well in control" when the fact was that only a small beachhead on an entire island had been secured. But that was all the area the Marines required to begin their push to clean out the island. For them, establishing the beachhead was the major obstacle to victory.

Adams related the strategy of the Marines to the Christian life. At conversion, God establishes a "beachhead" in the life of the believer (positional sanctification). And just as the Marines were never shoved off an island during the war, God's "beachhead" in the life of the believer is eternal. From this "beachhead," the Holy Spirit is welcome to work in the life of the believer and purge out the enemy (worldly and fleshly pursuits), thereby yielding more and more control to the Spirit of God (progressive sanctification).

Adams' illustration is a good one, but with one important difference—*time*. Progressive sanctification is not an overnight victory. While the Marines might overtake an island in a matter of weeks or months, the work of the Holy Spirit is a lifetime of personal, dedicated effort, culminating at our perfection in Christ when we meet Him face to face.

Growing Through Change

It's a fact that in our lifetime we'll need to adjust several times to new and different behavior and attitude swings within the family, church and culture. Ours is a transient and fleeting society—change is unavoidable. But this does not imply that we should ever compromise our values and beliefs.

Updates in traditional methods to meet contemporary needs are essential if the church is to grow and reach out to a dying world. According to Dr. Gary L. McIntosh of the Church Growth Network, the church of the '90s must develop new ministries, such as counseling services for divorce recovery and marital breakdowns, and support groups for combatting drugs, alcoholism and homosexuality. Worship services need to become positive, uplifting and contemporary, utilizing music, video and drama. [2]

It's important to note that while these changes are non-traditional, they are not non-biblical. In the midst of change, we need to be careful never to compromise the inerrant Word of God. We may have to adjust our methods, but never our practices. We must freely and continually yield to the Holy Spirit's work of renewing our mind so we will know the difference.

Our commitment to Christ is a lifetime obligation, not a short-term answer. Let's prepare ourselves for the long haul, if God wills, and "press on to maturity" (Hebrews 6:1).

For Reflection, Discussion and Action

1. In what ways have you treated your life in Christ as a short-term commitment?

2. Can you admit to some "Christian" habits which may be preventing you from viewing your walk with Christ in a long-term perspective?

3. Why do so many believers seem to struggle when pressured to conform to the world?

4. What measures have you taken in your life to help you put off any earthly desires which conflict with your life in Christ? Describe a few of them.

5. Is progressive sanctification at work in your life? How do you know?

6. What steps will you take to ensure your continual

willingness to yield to the Holy Spirit to renew
your mind in the midst of a changing world?

Part II

*Setting
the Pace*

6

Growing Strong in Our Weakness

My strength is made perfect in weakness
(2 Corinthians 12:9).

I remember watching on TV the stunning victory by Greg LeMond in the 1986 Tour De France bicycle race and thinking to myself, *I ought to start riding my bicycle again.* I hadn't really ridden my bike for some ten years, but I had always enjoyed the feeling of coasting down the road as the wind cut briskly through my hair.

So one day in September, I surprised Janet and dragged my old K Mart bike out of the garage, dusted it off and pumped up the tires. I then set out on a six-mile ride.

The first three miles were slightly down hill. With the wind at my back, I thought, *Hey, this feels pretty good!* But soon I turned a corner and faced my first hill. Nearing the top, I thought I was going to die. My legs were burning and my lungs couldn't get enough air.

Just as I reached the top, another bicyclist came up from behind and passed me like I was standing still. As he went by, he yelled, "Come on, let's stand on those pedals!" I was so tired, I could not respond. I got off my bike and tried to catch my breath. I felt embarrassed and miserable. Having been somewhat of an athlete in my high school days, I had a certain amount of pride in my physical endurance. His comment was particularly painful to me.

After a few minutes, I got on my bike and slowly rode home. All the way back, I kept thinking to myself how I wished I could have told that bicyclist that I was riding my bike for the first time in years. He then would have understood that I had not yet developed my cardiovascular conditioning or strengthened my leg muscles to ride up such a hill the way he did. With my pride bruised and battered (not to mention the way my entire body felt), I finally reached home where Janet greeted me with a friendly, "How was your ride, dear? I bet it felt great!"

In the few days that followed, I decided that if I was going to seriously ride my bike, I would need to get in shape. And to get into any kind of respectable condition, it would require from three to six months of consistent training. I decided to go for it.

While I was training, I made a promise that when I passed slower bicyclists, I would never make condescending remarks toward them since I didn't know their individual situations. My humiliating experience at the top of that hill taught me an important lesson: Without the facts, don't ever conclude that what appears to be true is true.

The Stigma of Strength

I think there is a lesson for believers here, especially for those who desire to grow deeper in their faith. The lesson is simply this: Don't let the strength of your faith go to your head; channel it through your heart. Let me explain.

I have watched "stronger" believers chide weaker believers to spiritually "grow up" and "mature." Sometimes the chiding is deserved. But often what happens is the critical attitude of the stronger believer only drives a deeper wedge between the two groups. Soon the weaker brother labels the stronger as self-righteous and arrogant while the stronger brother labels the weaker as carnal and lazy.

What is ironic about this is the fact that by virtue of his attitude, the so-called "stronger believer" is not strong at all! He merely thinks he is. In the eyes of God, though, he is no better off than the weaker brother: "For if anyone thinks he is something when he is nothing, he deceives himself" (Galatians 6:3).

Apparently, there were similar problems like this in the early church, especially between the Jewish and Gentile Christians. In the Book of Romans, Paul discusses believers who are both strong and weak in their faith:

> Now accept the one who is weak in faith, but not for the purpose of passing judgment on his opinions (Romans 14:1).
> Now we who are strong ought to bear the weakness of those without strength and not just please ourselves (Romans 15:1).

In the first verse, Paul states that the stronger brother must *accept* the weaker brother in regard to debatable issues. The weaker brother's faith may not be knowledgeable enough to perceive the full liberty he has in Christ. (In this instance, a weaker brother confined his diet to vegetables for fear of eating meat which might have been sacrificed to idols.) The weaker brother must not be made to feel inferior or second-rate if he misapplies his new understanding about the teachings of Christ.

In the second verse (15:1), Paul points out that it is the responsibility of the stronger believer to take the initiative to reach out in fellowship and support to the weaker brother. The stronger believer must not act in a spirit of pride and self-interest, but in love and gentleness.

In both of these verses, we can clearly see that the stronger believer has a definite responsibility toward the weaker brother. The stronger brother is to accept the weaker believer as well as *bear* his weaknesses.

Before we consider how we are to accept and bear the weaknesses of the weaker brother, we need to consider two very important questions:

1. What does "weak in faith" mean?

2. Who is weak and who is strong?

A Definition of "Weak"

What does Paul mean when he speaks about one who is "weak in faith?" Does he mean an individual who is spiritually immature as a result of merely being a new believer? Or does he mean a believer who chooses to mix his faith with works or compromises his faith with the beliefs of the world?

All indications seem to suggest that Paul is referring to a new believer. In both verses, Paul speaks in a tone of gentleness and even protection about those who are weak in faith. You never see Paul writing in such a kind and merciful manner for the believer who remains spiritually immature at his own choosing.

But then the second question arises: Who is weak

and who is strong? Should the length of time we know Christ be our standard of measure? Probably not. The truth is, we are all strong in some areas and weak in others. Let me suggest what I believe to be the biblical standard of measure.

An area in our lives which does not fall into sin when it is touched by sin reveals our strength in that area. And an area which falls into sin when touched by it reveals our weakness. For example, a believer who has the ability to resist the love of money reveals the strength of his faith to believe that God will supply all his needs. Yet this same believer's inability to resist a lustful thought resulting in sin reveals the weakness of his faith to trust God to provide a way of escape from the temptation (1 Corinthians 10:13).

The stronger believer is essentially the one who is able to resist sin in more areas of his life. His faith allows him to yield control of his life to the Holy Spirit and subject himself to the authority of the Holy Spirit. As a result, this promise of God is fulfilled: "But I say, walk by the Spirit, and you will not carry out the desire of the flesh" (Galatians 5:16).

Accepting the Weaker Brother

Fellowship between strong and weak believers is a major source of struggle among Christians. Though the new believer is gratefully accepted into the body of Christ, often he is not included in the inner circle of stronger believers. I experienced this first hand.

About three months after my conversion to Christ, I started attending a college youth group at a local evangelical church. The group was quite large and had plenty of quality Bible studies and social activities to keep us busy. Two of our leaders, Mark and Gary, were energetic and inspirational. Their lives seemed very spiritual and sincere. I always enjoyed talking with them and learning all I could from their Bible studies.

In my relationship with them, however, something always nagged at me. Though I tried to fit in, they never made much of an effort to include me in their inner circle of fellowship. Of course, there was always a handshake and a "Hi, how are ya," at church, but that was the end of it. They seemed happy that I was a part of "their group," but they never invited me to their home or included me in any of the after-church lunches they would often arrange with some of the "stronger" believers.

That winter our group had a three-day retreat in the mountains north of San Bernardino, California. I roomed with four guys who were all considered "strong" believers and a part of the inner circle of fellowship and leadership with Mark and Gary.

One fellow was a guy I had gone to high school with, but we really didn't know each other since we had spent our high school years on opposite sides of the social spectrum. You see, I had played football and run in a crowd that did not care much for academics. Dwight, on the other hand, had been a top student who had played the bagpipes in the school band. In my high school years, I had very little respect for anyone who played the bagpipes! But there we were, rooming together for three days and our only common bond was our love for Christ.

To my surprise, Dwight was the only one of the four guys who made an earnest effort to get to know me. And even though I was not a part of their inner circle, he would personally include me. Dwight made me feel like a genuine part of the family of God. He sincerely cared about me.

Well to say the least, my opinion of Dwight, and even his bagpipes, drastically changed. Despite the fact that he and I had come out of two different worlds, it was he—and not our two leaders—who taught me all about the Pauline principle of the stronger brother accepting the weaker brother. He never criticized or judged me. He did not look down on my spiritual immaturity, and he was always tolerant of my youthful and sometimes misplaced spiritual enthusiasm. He, more than any sermon or Bible study, showed me the ideal of Christian acceptance without reservation. And not surprisingly, we became the best of friends—a relationship which is still going strong after eighteen years.

Our willingness to accept another believer should never be a conditional decision based on the degree of maturity. Rather, we should behave as if we are accepting Christ Himself:

> For I was hungry, and you gave Me something to eat; I was thirsty, and you gave Me drink; I was a stranger, and you invited Me in; naked, and you clothed Me; I was sick, and you visited Me; I was in prison, and you came to Me.... Truly I say to you, to the extent that you did it to one of these brothers of Mine, even the least of them, you did it to Me (Matthew 25:35,36,40b).

As you grow in Christ, do not lose sight of your weaker brother and sister. Accept them as Christ accepted you when you were new and immature in the faith. Remember Christ's example. The impression you imprint might be the only "gospel" some people will ever see.

Bearing the Weaknesses of the Weaker Brother

One of the great church fathers of the second century was Tertullian. He once wrote: "It is our care for the helpless, our practicing of lovingkindness, that brands us in the eyes of our opponents. 'Look,' they say, 'how they love one another. Look how they are prepared to die for one another!' "

It would have been exciting to live in Tertullian's day. Imagine living for Christ with such a passion, that to die for Him or for our fellow believer would not be a difficult decision to make. We would proudly declare without hesitation:

> I count all things to be loss in view of the surpassing value of knowing Christ Jesus my Lord, for whom I have suffered the loss of all things, and count them but rubbish in order that I may gain Christ (Philippians 3:8).

But we are not living in Tertullian's day, and you don't have to look much farther than today's American teenagers to realize that fact. Without a doubt, this generation of young people are among the most self-absorbed and self-centered youth I have seen throughout my eighteen years of working with teens. Anthony Campolo, in his provocative book *Growing Up In America*, cites a comment by Christopher Lasch:

> Middle-class American teenagers are definitely part of the "me generation"; their neurotic self-interest has led many social scientists to believe they may constitute the most egotistical generation in the history of Western culture.[1]

Campolo adds:

> Research on contemporary high school students reveals that they have few, if any, concerns beyond their own immediate world.
>
> Careful analysis reveals that even young people's seemingly altruistic activities are carried out more to feel good or to attract attention to how

wonderful they are than from a deep concern for the needs of others.[2]

How have our youth come to the point of leading such egocentric lives? Most likely it is a result of the secularization of the family and our cultural values. Our society has been affected by the demands prompted by consumerism and competition. Material needs have become our priority.

In the quest for the almighty dollar, mom and dad have lost their desire to care for the concerns of others—including their own children. Consequently, their children, in order to manufacture a sense of self-worth, become obsessed with fulfilling their own needs. They, in turn, lose their desire to care for the concerns of others. It is no wonder that a generation of believers might naturally overlook the need to bear the weaknesses of fellow believers.

Bearing weaknesses of others will demand our time and effort. It is at this point where the truths of God may disrupt our habits and challenge our desire to grow strong in Christ. Growing closer to Christ requires a willingness to help and encourage the weak and the fainthearted. According to the law of Christ, we are to love one another (John 13:34) and bear one another's burdens (Galatians 6:2).

Look for occasions to take a weaker believer out to lunch or dinner. Offer to involve yourself in a discipling relationship with him.[3] Consider areas in your local church ministry where you could affect the lives of those who are struggling in their faith. There are a number of things you could do to actively bear the weaknesses of your fellow Christians.

Don't allow your growth in Christ to put you out of

reach of weaker believers. They, more than anyone else, will need your help along the way.

For Reflection, Discussion and Action

1. Can the strength of one's faith breed spiritual pride? In what ways?

2. How do you perceive a person who is weak in faith? Do you tend to want to pray for him or neglect him? Why?

3. Name some areas of faith in your life which are strong and some that are weak. What could you do to strengthen the weaker areas?

4. Name some specific ways that you can tangibly accept the weaker brother.

5. Name some specific ways that you can tangibly bear the weaknesses of a weaker brother.

6. If possible, write down the name of a person who needs encouragement in his/her faith. What do you intend to do?

7

Developing Into a Domestique

But the greatest among you shall be your servant (Matthew 23:11).

Le domestique is a French term for a team bicycle racer whose sole job is to work and sacrifice himself for the good of the team. Each team has nine riders: Two or three are considered team leaders while the rest serve as *domestiques.*

The *domestique's* role is hardly a glamorous one. He is expected to sacrifice himself for his team leaders by leading their way and breaking the wind for them. He is responsible to deliver food, drink and instructions from the team car to the leaders. And he is required to make the ultimate sacrifice: to give up his bicycle should a team leader's bike break down during the race. The *domestique* will do whatever he can to help his team on to victory.

In a sense, Christ served as a *domestique* for all mankind. His death on the cross is the ultimate example of sacrifice and servanthood. As believers, we are commanded to have the mind of Christ (1 Corinthians 2:15,16) and to practice His ways (Philippians 3:17; 4:9). Yet many of us struggle at naturally displaying a servant's heart. It is difficult for us to become full-time *domestiques* for our fellow brothers and sisters in Christ. We balk at the thought of complete servanthood. Perhaps we want the glory of serving as chiefs, but do not want to put in our time as Indians.

This is often true within Christian leadership. Time and time again I have seen believers who love to be recognized as strong and faithful leaders, but are seldom found working in the church nursery or vacuuming the carpets.

Not surprisingly, Jesus addressed a similar matter with the disciples. Matthew 20 relates an almost humorous event involving James, John and their mother:

> Then the mother of the sons of Zebedee came to Him with her sons, bowing down, and making a request of Him. And He said to her, "What do you wish?" She said to Him, "Command that in Your Kingdom these two sons of mine may sit, one on Your right and one on Your left." But Jesus answered and said, "You do not know what you are asking for. Are you able to drink the cup that I am about to drink?" They said to Him, "We are able." He said to them, "My cup you shall drink; but to sit on My right and on My left, this is not Mine to give, but it is for those for whom it has been prepared by My Father" (Matthew 20:20-23).

The mother of James and John had asked Jesus to give her sons special positions in His Kingdom. Unfortunately, she and her sons had failed to understand the Lord's previous teachings about rewards (19:16-30) as well as eternal life (20:1-16). They had also failed to understand that they would have to pay a price and suffer for Christ before living in the glory of the Kingdom of God (the "cup" represented the suffering and crucifixion of Christ).

Jesus responded by declaring that He was subject to the authority of the Father and any decision about leadership in heaven was made by God. Furthermore, such rewards of leadership were not given as favors but granted as a result of a believer's commitment to Christ in spite of the trials he faced.

This is not the end of the story, however. After hearing of this, the rest of the disciples became upset with James and John. They felt that James and John were pushing for the top spots in heaven. While this was true, the rest of the disciples did, in fact, want the same thing for themselves. They wanted to be at the top with Christ. They were not interested in service or servanthood. They were interested in glory.

Knowing their hearts, Jesus put all of them in their rightful place. He outlines the requirements for such a position:

> You know that the rulers of the Gentiles lord it over them, and their great men exercise authority over them. It is not so among you, but whoever wishes to become great among you shall be your servant, and whoever wishes to be first among you shall be your slave; just as the Son of Man did not come to be served, but to serve, and to give His life a ransom for many (Matthew 20:25-28).

Jesus viewed leadership from a completely new perspective—from that of being a servant. After rebuking the disciples for their selfishness, he explained that in order to be recognized as leaders—spiritually mature leaders—they must develop the willingness and the ability to be a servant to those they "rule." Such a concept was completely foreign to the disciples.

It is very easy for a growing believer to inadvertently assume a sense of spiritual pride or even conceit. After all, when he compares his personal sacrifice and commitment to the weaker believers around him, he could very easily begin to view himself as a "better Christian" and develop a spiritual attitude not unlike James and John. Once in this mindset, a believer may have to be taught a very difficult lesson in order to understand the true meaning of biblical servanthood. Let me illustrate.

A friend of mine served as the youth minister in a large church. In a couple of years, his ministry had grown to become one of the largest youth groups in our area.

In the middle of what seemed to be a very productive ministry, Ken was abruptly fired. The day after his firing, he phoned me with the bad news and asked for prayer. Offering my sympathy, yet baffled about his firing, I softly questioned him about it.

Ken told me that he felt the leadership of the church was not interested in growth because they were not interested in some of his new ideas. He thought they lacked the spiritual maturity to lead the church. Because of those feelings, there was a sharp disagreement between Ken and the elder board—and he was relieved of his duties.

It hurts me when I hear of a brother in the ministry getting fired, regardless of the circumstances. There will always be a great amount of pain suffered by both parties. I was once unceremoniously relieved of my duties, even though my life and my heart were pure and above reproach before man and God. I experienced periods of dejection and depression for months. From that perspective, I empathized with Ken.

But I felt I needed to hear both sides of the story, so I met with several of Ken's elders. After our meeting, I realized that the problem was not what Ken had surmised. His elders were godly, caring men who only wanted God's best for their church. They were not out to "get" Ken or rebuke his new ideas. Rather, it was Ken who had begun recently to display an arrogant and prideful spirit toward the leadership. He had expressed several condescending remarks to his youth group about the pastor and the elders. When questioned about it, Ken abruptly accused the elders of spiritual immaturity and declared himself as one of the few strong believers in the church. He further claimed that because God was blessing his ministry, his feelings about the elders must be accurate.

The success of Ken's ministry fueled his ego and his spiritual pride. Consequently, he began to view himself above the ordained leadership of his church and refused to submit to their authority.

Becoming strong in his own eyes caused him to lose sight of being a servant first and then a leader. Whatever understanding Ken had about servanthood had become self-serving and restrictive. As a result, the Lord was forced to teach him a very painful lesson about servanthood—a lesson he needed to learn if he was going to continue serving the people of God in another ministry.

Three Aspects to Servanthood

Does our profession of faith in Christ automatically produce a servant's heart in us? Do we instantaneously become a humble, gentle person who impeccably displays a submissive spirit? Not hardly. A servant's heart is produced only as we willfully choose to be led by the Holy Spirit and exhibit His fruit (see Galatians 5:18,22,23).

But how do we practically exhibit a servant's heart? Do we assist another brother financially? Do we bring a needy family a cooked meal every now and then? Do we offer to regularly cut the widow's lawn down our street? Just what marks a person as a true servant of God? The character of servanthood is probably best illustrated by these three important truths:

1. We must fulfill every condition of God's Word in order to serve Him effectively.

2. Accomplishing work for God is not the same as serving Him.

3. A servant expects nothing in return.

1. We must fulfill every condition of God's Word in order to serve Him effectively.

While this aspect of our service may not be new to most believers, I believe it is often overlooked. In order to be an effective servant of God, we cannot neglect even the most minor instruction we receive from God's Word. Often, serving God in some capacity causes us to think of ourselves as too important and vital to His plans. Consequently, we lapse in our observation of His instructions and end up obeying only what we feel is necessary for us.

Consider Moses. He responded to God's call to lead His people out of Egypt, yet neglected to fulfill the conditions of the Law which stipulated that his son be circumcised. If Zipporah had not jumped in at the last second to circumcise her son, the Lord would have put Moses to death (Exodus 4:22-26). Moses' service to God would have promptly ended.

We must never assume that we are above the Law and have the right to pick and choose only the truths of God's Word that we want to observe. That's like saying that because we have an understanding about computers, we do not need to follow the instructions in assembling one. Without directions, we are bound to make a mistake or miss a step in the process. The Scriptures have been given to us for our complete instruction (2 Timothy 3:16) and are not to be viewed as incomplete or partially applicable.

There is no doubt in my mind that failure to understand this point leads to heretical teachings. A leader becomes so powerful that he assumes he has a right to interpret Scripture only to fit his purposes. He is no longer a servant of God, but a servant unto himself—and God will judge accordingly (James 4:17).

Let us be on guard that we not spoil our ability to serve our Creator by refusing to observe all His truths and conditions.

2. Accomplishing work for God is not the same as serving Him.

In 2 Kings 10 we read about a king who accomplished great things for God, but was never His true servant.

Jehu was appointed by Elijah to replace Ahab as king of Israel. As king, Jehu was commanded by God to eradicate Baal worship throughout the Northern Kingdom. But even though Jehu boasted a zeal for God (2 Kings 10:16), his heart was not totally right with God (verse 31).

Because of political reasons, Jehu refused to destroy the calf-idol worship initiated by Jeroboam at Bethel and Dan. If he had destroyed those idols, worshippers would have gone to the Southern Kingdom to worship in the Temple.

While Jehu honored God by destroying Baal worship in Israel, he refused to destroy *all* idols for fear of losing his political clout. Thus, his heart was divided between his political aspirations and his "love" for God. He lacked a true servant's heart.

Having a servant's heart is not displayed by what we *do*, but by what we *are*. I believe this is perhaps one of the most misunderstood aspects of servanthood in the church today. Why? Because many Christians seem to think like an entrepreneur when it comes to service. The church provides the blessings through worship and we feel obligated to return the favor by offering our time and effort in performing various tasks.

But here's the problem: Loyalty is not measured solely by the amount of our sacrifice. For example, one man can give $10,000 to the offering and ten Saturdays a year to working around the church. Yet this same man can be heard screaming obscenities at his employees to make himself feel more important Monday through Friday. He has divided loyalties. He displays a servant's heart around the church, but fails miserably as a servant to his unbelieving co-workers.

Another man may not give $10,000, but his complete loyalty and steadfastness to the truths of God set his life apart. His actions are characterized by a loving, giving, caring and sharing spirit regardless of his circumstance or predicament. He can be counted on to respond to needs as Christ would.

The prophet Hosea recorded these powerful words describing what God is looking for from us: "For I delight in loyalty rather than sacrifice, and in the knowledge of God rather than burnt offerings" (Hosea 6:6).

Ask yourself these questions: Do I serve God "part-time" and not consistently out of a heart of love? Do I have divided loyalties which cause me to serve conditionally?

Embracing a biblical view of service means that we live a consistent lifestyle honoring to God and of faithful service to the needs of man—unconditionally.

3. A servant expects nothing in return.

Between his second and third birthday, our eldest son, Ryan, often struggled to eat his meals. Though we understood his behavior as normal for a child his age, we still had a house rule that stated there were no desserts for the person who did not finish his meal. (This rule came back to haunt us. One evening a guest at our table did not finish her meal, causing Ryan to loudly declare, "No dessert for you. You did not finish your dinner!")

Every now and then, though, Ryan would finish his meal and happily smile as he asked for his dessert of "Fruit Wrinkles." He was very proud of his accomplishment.

I remember the first time he finished his meal and discovered there were no more Fruit Wrinkles. He cried and cried and cried while clinging to our legs, hoping that we would somehow produce dessert. He was simply devastated that his accomplishment had not been rewarded.

Like my son at his young age, the immature believer insists on a reward for his services. He struggles with the idea of doing or performing a needed task without any recognition or compensation.

Interestingly, as Ryan grew older and more mature, rewards for finishing his meal—or accomplishing any task—became less of a concern. He slowly learned that doing something good didn't require a reward.

Likewise, a mature servant of God will not expect anything in return for his "good deeds." Rather, his work is motivated purely out of a heart of love for God. He understands the selfless sacrifice Jesus made on his behalf and is therefore glad to offer what services he can give without a thought of demanding an earthly reward.

A true, selfless servant of God understands that "every good thing bestowed and every perfect gift is from above" (James 1:17), and is given at His appointed time, not ours. We, indeed, shall receive rewards for our work

(Exodus 39:43; 2 Corinthians 9:10-12; 1 Peter 5:9-11; 2 Peter 1:11), but such rewards must never serve as our only motivation for our work. Our motivation for service is to be a direct result of our desire to glorify God.

I believe that the closer you draw to God, the more you will develop a servant's heart. One day we will stand before Him, and what a joy it will be to hear, "Well done, good and faithful servant!" (Matthew 25:21, NIV)

Ian Maclaren once said, "The world cannot always understand one's profession of faith, but it can understand service."

For Reflection, Discussion and Action

1. Name some *domestique* believers in your church. What sets them apart?

2. In what ways have you struggled in serving others? What specifically makes service a struggle for you?

3. Is your ability to serve God being hindered because there are some conditions in the Word of God that you are neglecting to observe? If so, why not confess them before God right now?

4. Are there any areas of your life that you thought were a service to God, but now, after reading this chapter, you realize they are not? What could you do to change that?

5. Name some acts of recent service in which you quietly looked for something in return. How did you respond when you received nothing?

6. Make a list of at least five acts of service you would like to accomplish freely over the next three months.

8

Considering Our Conduct

Truly I say to you, unless you are converted and
become like children, you shall not enter the
kingdom of heaven (Matthew 18:3).

A few years ago, a pastor friend of mine in a neigh-
boring church was arrested for drunk driving. In the
midst of depression and fatigue, he left his house late one
night, purchased a large quantity of liquor and drank it
while driving around the city for several hours. His
drunken spree finally ended when his car collided with
a parked car and a tree. He was immediately arrested and
spent the night in jail.

David was a man of God who had the deep respect
of his congregation as well as many officials in the community. He had always been very stable and never
showed any signs of irrational or compulsive behavior.
But the pressure of his pastorate combined with some
difficulties at home caused him in a moment's rush to do
something totally out of character. It not only shocked his
congregation, but also upset the entire community.

Unfortunately for David, as well as for the cause of
Christ in the area, the next day brought angry denuncia-

tions and protests in the town newspaper. One writer suggested that such an incident would not be so sensational if Christians would not act so arrogantly self-righteous toward non-Christians. The criticisms were not only pointing at David, but at the entire Christian community as well.

David underwent church discipline and counseling, and is now effectively serving the Lord again in another state. But the effects of his actions on that fateful night still linger in the church and in the community.

To say such a situation is disappointing to God is an understatement. Yet most of us do not need to look very far before we hear of other similar occurrences involving "strong" believers who fell to immorality, public fraud or financial dishonesty. The results have been disastrous.

The church is no longer considered a moral force in the community. Civic leaders no longer check with church leadership in regard to community moral and ethical issues. Where there once was a thriving evangelistic message that reached deep into the non-believing community, Christianity has now taken a back seat to the values and standards of a humanistic world. There does not seem to be much hope of change in the near future.

In this chapter, we are going to focus on the importance of maintaining an excellent testimony as part of our deeper growth in the faith. We have been given the urgent responsibility to carry the gospel into the world—and so we should.

But often, it is what we *do* rather than what we *say* that determines whether our message is accepted and understood. It has been said that one believer who displays a poor example of Christ will do more harm than a thousand non-believers cursing the faith.

Ambassadors of Christ

Believers pursuing a deeper walk with Christ need to understand that their lives will fall under closer scrutiny than ever before. They will be watched and evaluated as others look for cracks in the armor.

Such scrutiny should not come as a big surprise, though. Jesus told us that the world will hate us (John 15:18-23). And Peter warned that Satan "prowls about like a roaring lion, seeking someone to devour" (1 Peter 5:8). As believers, we are targets for Satan's fiery darts, and I firmly believe that the stronger and more visible our stand for Christ, the larger the target we become.

We learn in 2 Corinthians that believers are "ambassadors for Christ" (2 Corinthians 5:20). An ambassador is an official representative from one country to another. We are representatives of Christ to a lost world.

How does a person represent his or her country? Does he merely show up at social functions, offering short speeches about the state of his country? No, it goes much further than that. Everything from an ambassador's attire to his favorite hobby serve to represent his country.

As believers, do we represent Christ in our neighborhood merely by attending church every Sunday? Do we display Christ simply by decorating our house with religious ornaments each Christmas? No, it requires much more as well.

Just as an ambassador represents his country by everything he does, believers in Jesus Christ represent Him—whether we like it or not—in everything we do.

Several years ago I had a young girl in my high school group who claimed to love the Lord. But Diana struggled with the idea that Christians were not to love the things of this world or deeply associate themselves with worldly individuals. As a result, she would often get in trouble with her parents or school officials by cutting classes, getting poor grades or being caught with the wrong kids in the smoking pit behind the school. It got to be such a problem that she was almost told to leave school.

Unfortunately, Diana did not see anything wrong with running around with a group of ungodly kids. Consequently, she was easily influenced by their actions. Scripture has much to say about who we associate with (1 Corinthians 15:33; 2 Timothy 3; James 4:4). There is always the possibility that in a time of weakness, we can be led astray. In Diana's case, this was frequently the result.

In her defense, Diana would attempt to justify her actions by saying that God would always keep her from falling into some drastic temptation (citing 1 Corinthians 10:13). But if she did fall, God would forgive her and everything would be fine.

Well, there is a lot we could say about her application of Scripture, but one of her major problems was that she failed to recognize how her disobedient and unruly actions spoiled her testimony as a Christian—especially in the eyes of the rebellious crowd she hung around with.

Almost a year later, a young man who knew Diana at school trusted Christ in his life. He soon became involved in our youth group and became active in my discipleship program. One day after Sunday school, he came down to my office with a startled look on his face. "Do you know who came to Sunday school this morning?" he asked. I said that I had peeked in but had not noticed anyone in particular. "Diana was in Sunday school!" he exclaimed. And he added, "She even prayed!"

I told him that Diana had been coming to our group

for three years, even though her attendance was irregular. Hearing this, he looked surprised and confused. He knew Diana in school but never had the slightest idea that she was a Christian or even went to church. In fact, he said, her lifestyle had influenced him away from God and the church for more than a year.

Once we make the claim that we are Christians, we have a tremendous responsibility to exhibit Christ in order to bring glory to Him, not embarrassment. Satan will claim victory any time he can dent the cause of Christ by distorting the testimony of one of God's ambassadors.

The Evil "Little" Sin

Though we shouldn't rely on any man for our spiritual growth, imagine how devastated thousands, maybe millions, would be if Billy Graham were to fall into some gross sin. We have already felt the censure of the world because a few well-known evangelists have soiled their testimony.

But is falling into gross sin the only way we can hurt our testimony? Is it just the "big" sins that do the damage? I think many Christians feel that if they can get away with committing "little" sins without distorting their testimony, then they can still live the Christian life without guilt. The major problem with this (not to mention sin is sin in God's eyes—regardless of how "bad" it is) is the fact that "small" sins invariably lead to "larger" sins. Why? Because committing the smaller sins did not negatively affect our conscience. Without our conscience notifying us of wrong moves, we become increasingly lenient and careless.

Such was the case with Lot, Abraham's nephew. As a result of strife between the herdsmen of Abraham and Lot, Abraham offered Lot his choice of land so that he and Lot would be separated. Lot selfishly chose the Valley of the Jordan, which consisted of the cities of Sodom and Gomorrah.

Lot could not resist the temptation that Sodom offered. Eventually, he moved his tent into the center of the city and became involved in its sinful activities. Fortunately for Lot, God chose to deliver him before He destroyed Sodom. Lot's "small" sins of pride and selfishness led him to "larger" sins which nearly cost him his life.

Lot's example contains a warning: Never consider yourself beyond sin's potential grip—no matter how strong you may feel in Christ. Confess every "small" sin before God—before it overcomes you.

Keeping Our Behavior Excellent

Scripture reveals three specific areas we must guard against Satan. He wants nothing more than to lead us astray and bring shame on our testimony in Jesus Christ. If it is our desire to seek a deeper relationship with Christ, we must be mindful of each of these areas in our daily walk:

1. What we say (Titus 2:6-8).

2. What we do (1 Peter 2:12).

3. What we think (1 Peter 3:16).

1. What We Say (Titus 2:6-8)

In the middle of the seventeenth century, an author by the name of Theodore Reinking faced execution because he had offended King Christian IV of Denmark with a book he had written. But King Christian was merciful and offered Reinking an alternative to his execution. Instead of being put to death, he told Reinking he could save his life if he would eat his book. Taking the king up on his offer, Reinking promptly tore the book into shreds and soaked it in soup. He then munched away until he devoured the entire book.

Most of us are not as fortunate as Reinking. Once we speak, our words are forever a part of our eternal record. The apostle Paul understood how critical our words are, especially in regard to the kingdom of God. In Titus 2, Paul reminded young Titus how the choice of his words can shut the mouths of critics:

> Likewise urge the young men to be sensible; in all things show yourself to be an example of good deeds, with purity in doctrine, dignified, sound in speech which is above reproach, in order that the opponent may be put to shame, having nothing bad to say about us (Titus 2:6-8).

Even though Titus was a strong believer in Christ, Paul felt it necessary to remind him that his words can either be a help or a hindrance to the gospel. Sensible and reasonable conversation will not give an opponent anything to criticize or judge.

All too often non-believers tell me that one reason they are not Christians is because they hear Christians talk like non-believers, using abusive language and gossiping about others. I have to admit that I, too, would be doubtful if I was told that Christ will make a difference in a person's life, yet the Christian's language is no different from mine. What is this Jesus going to do for me that He apparently cannot do in the lives of these Christians?

James accurately describes the tongue as a fire that can defile the entire body (James 3:6). A believer's loose tongue can easily put to shame any testimony, any respect he may have built up in the eyes of those around him. We don't want to stump our growth in Christ by not controlling what we say or how we say it. Remember the words of Jesus:

> And I say to you, that every careless word that men shall speak, they shall render account for it in the day of judgment. For by your words you shall be justified, and by your words you shall be condemned (Matthew 12:36,37).

2. What We Do (1 Peter 2:12)

Billy Graham tells the story of a Hindu student who once told him that he would become a Christian if he could see one. Graham said, "And when he said that to me, he was looking right at me! That was one of the greatest sermons ever preached to me."

Indeed, our actions speak very loudly about who we are. If we have Christ in our life, our actions must speak of Him. But if we draw nearer to God only in our mind and not our heart, our actions may become too obvious or self-righteous. That was the problem with the Pharisees in Jesus' day. Their only desire was to show off their lengthy tassels and wide phylacteries (Matthew 23:5). They had become so self-righteous that there was no meaningful reverence or personal humbleness in their service to God. Their actions resulted from a selfish attitude and a prideful, arrogant spirit.

It is possible for a believer sincerely pursuing a deeper relationship with Christ to become so spiritually pious that he inadvertently develops a condescending or offensive attitude—especially toward non-believers. Young or immature believers who suddenly view themselves as spiritual giants are particularly susceptible.

A greater amount of knowledge often breeds a certain degree of confidence—perhaps more accurately called "arrogance." I believe this is one of the major reasons the Bible instructs us not to put a new believer in a leadership position too soon. The humility and patience of Christ is not learned through head knowledge, but over time through experience and the growth process. As we grow closer to God, we will understand more and more of His character. But until we can actually *appropriate* His character in our lives on a consistent basis, our understanding may result in temporary bursts of righteousness intended only to feed our spiritual egos at the proper times.

Such "Christian" character is killing the cause of Christ. Peter writes:

> Keep your behavior excellent among the Gentiles, so that in the thing in which they slander you as evildoers, they may on account of your good deeds, as they observe them, glorify God in the day of visitation (1 Peter 2:12).

I recently came across some notes I had taken while listening to a Bible teacher many years ago at a retreat. In fact, it was so long ago, I do not remember who the teacher was. But his message concluded with how we ought to walk. We are to:

Walk in newness of life (Romans 6:4).

Walk in honesty (2 Corinthians 8:21).

Walk in the Spirit (Galatians 5:16).

Walk worthy of our calling (Ephesians 4:1).

Walk in love (Ephesians 5:2).

Walk as children of light (Ephesians 5:8).

Walk as wise men (Ephesians 5:15).

Walk worthy of the Lord (Colossians 1:10).

Walk worthy of God (1 Thessalonians 2:12).

Walk pleasing to God (1 Thessalonians 4:1).

Walk as He walked (1 John 2:6).

3. What We Think (1 Peter 3:16)

Controlling what we think is probably the hardest thing to do. Our actions are a direct result of what we are thinking. Peter reminds us to act so that our conscience is clear:

> And keep a good conscience so that in the thing in which you are slandered, those who revile your good behavior in Christ may be put to shame (1 Peter 3:16).

Peter knew that our conscience always speaks the loudest to us *after* our actions. Thus, good actions will result in a clear conscience.

Believers desiring to grow stronger in the faith need to become more "conscience-minded," thereby encouraging godly actions. But as we saw earlier, there is a danger of thinking too highly of ourselves which may result in piously arrogant behavior.

I believe a key to prevent this from happening is having a proper perception of ourselves before God. Do we see ourselves as a select group of bold believers who are being used mightily by God to win the world? Or do we see ourselves as broken, yet loved and humble, children who are privileged to represent Christ in a world of pain and suffering? Our answer is found in Philippians:

> Do nothing from selfishness or empty conceit, but with humility of mind let each of you regard one another as more important than himself; do not merely look out for your own personal interests, but also for the interests of others. Have this attitude in yourselves which was also in Christ Jesus (Philippians 2:3-5).

As a pastor, I struggle with this concept. Being in a position of leadership like the pastorate (which, in itself, promotes a sense of pride and confidence), a pastor often has difficulty balancing strength with weakness. On one hand, he is supposed to lead his congregation in confidence and strength. On the other hand, he is supposed to be humble and gentle—having the attitude which was in Christ Jesus (Philippians 2:5). All too often, the pastor assumes the stronger, even dictatorial role which polarizes his congregation and tends to neglect the weak and needy—not to mention what happens to those who choose to oppose him. Consequently, his work becomes a work in the flesh and is doomed to fail (Romans 2:8,9).

But it is not just pastors who are susceptible to such behavior. Indeed, any position of authority within the church can promote such an attitude. It is our responsibility to remind ourselves daily to walk as Christ walked (1 John 2:6). At least five times in the New Testament we are told to humble *ourselves* and God will exalt us.

Indeed, there are cautions to be heeded if we choose to step out a little closer to God. The enemy will do all he can to hinder our relationship by discrediting us. Let's make it difficult on him by measuring what we say, do and think according to God's standards.

For Reflection, Discussion and Action

1. How is your personal testimony viewed in your neighborhood? Is Christianity respected as a result of your behavior?

2. Can you recall a time before you knew Christ when you thought most Christians were hypocrites? What caused you to think that way?

3. Are there any "little" sins in your life that could be

distorting your testimony to others? Spend some time with God and ask Him to reveal these sins to you. Then seek God's forgiveness and re-establish a testimony that is honoring to Him. If possible, share your discoveries with a close friend and ask him or her to continue to observe your life for signs of these "little" sins rearing their ugly heads again.

4. Write down something you said or did in the last six months that may have hurt your testimony before others. What did you do to rectify it?

5. Write down something you said or did in the last six months that glorified God before the world in which you live.

6. Do you have a clear conscience? If not, I suggest you put this book down and clear things up—both before God and man.

9

The Sufficiency of Christ

Set your mind on the things above, not on the things that are on the earth (Colossians 3:2).

Just a mile west of my office stands Lookout Mountain, gateway to the Rocky Mountains. It rises 1,300 feet above the city of Golden, Colorado. A winding road traverses five miles from its base to its summit at an average gradient of 12 percent.

It is a favorite road for bicycle enthusiasts. Bicyclists such as myself dare to climb it simply for the purpose of recording the time it takes to ride from its base to the entrance of "Wild Bill Cody's Grave" at the top. A bicyclist who has done some training can reach the top in thirty minutes.

One afternoon I decided to climb Lookout Mountain, but not with my twenty-one pound racing bike. I took my forty pound son, Ryan, sitting in the child's seat attached to my wife's thirty-four pound bicycle. It turned out to be a very interesting and painful experience.

As Ryan and I climbed the mountain, some bicyclists passed us, saying things like, "You guys are crazy!" "What a way to babysit!" "Boy, that'll get ya in shape!" I was too tired to respond and Ryan was enjoying himself and the view too much to be concerned about what other bicyclists were saying. He seemed even less concerned about his ol' dad who was sweating profusely and laboring on the pedals.

After thirty-five minutes we finally reached the top. I pulled off the road and drank the entire contents of my water bottle as Ryan kept nudging me, saying, "Come on, Daddy, let's do it again. Let's do it again!"

Two days later I did do it again. But this time, I was by myself on my racing bike. My time for the climb was just under twenty-five minutes.

What made me go faster? Obviously it was the fact that I was carrying a lot less weight—some fifty pounds less! Whenever I do a hill climb or a century ride, I carry the least amount of weight possible. The less weight, the more energy I'll preserve for the end of the ride.

Growing Strong and Losing Weight

The Scriptures clearly lay out for us the way in which we are to conduct our lives in Christ. But often, man comes along and adds his traditions, ceremonies and requirements in order to supplement his view or understanding of Scripture. What he adds merely becomes excess baggage that will invariably weigh down a believer to the point of burnout or disillusionment.

Just as my bike ride with my son slowed my time and spent my energy, a believer convinced that he must accomplish a number of additional requirements (beyond what Scripture teaches) in order to mature in Christ will, at best, labor in his efforts. Consider the Lord's faithful promise to us:

Come to Me, all who are weary and heavy-laden, and I will give you rest. Take My yoke upon you, and learn from Me, for I am gentle and humble in heart; and you shall find rest for your souls. For My yoke is easy, and My load is light (Matthew 11:28-30).

The idea of adding additional teachings and requirements to the Christian life is not new. Paul's letter to the Colossians, written while he was imprisoned in Rome, reveals that similar heresies had invaded the early Church.

The book relates the story about the pastor at the church of Colossae who was forced to go to the apostle Paul for help. The problem in Colossae was *syncretism*—a combination of ideas from other religions and philosophies that were challenging the belief that Christ was God and Savior. It caused immature Christians to believe that they needed to do more to prove or grow in their faith. Doing "more" included adhering to Jewish legalistic practices, Greek philosophical requirements and various Eastern mystical customs.

Believers are facing similar heresies today. Whether it be Christ *plus* a certain duty or practice, or Christ *plus* another "Scripture" or belief, many Christians are being taught to add additional requirements or tasks to what is mentioned in the Bible in order to "fulfill" their faith.

Sincere believers who seek a closer walk with God are particularly vulnerable to this type of religious quackery. I often hear disastrous stories of how growing Christians were led to believe that they must do, give or perform various things in order to be right with God. Whether it's the atrocities of a Jim Jones or the subtle inferences from an organization that giving will make you a better Christian, be on guard. Don't be misled that you must do more than what the Scriptures require to be closer to God.

With Colossians as our guide, let's take a look at the heresies mentioned by the apostle Paul in view of our society and culture today:

1. Humanistic philosophy (Colossians 2:1-10).

2. Legalism (Colossians 2:11-17).

3. Mysticism (Colossians 2:18,19).

4. Asceticism (Colossians 2:20-23).

1. Humanistic Philosophy (Colossians 2:1-10)

Essentially, humanistic philosophy is truth based entirely on man's perspective. There is no God—at least not in the biblical sense. Man is considered to be at the center of his universe. The apostle Paul directly warned the Colossians to beware of man's philosophies invading and twisting the truths about Jesus Christ:

> See to it that no one takes you captive through philosophy and empty deception, according to the tradition of men, according to the elementary prin- ciples of the world, rather than according to Christ (Colossians 2:8).

How is humanistic philosophy affecting us today? Quite clearly, the New Age movement is invading our schools, homes and churches in a lightning-fast manner.[1] Recognized "scientific" techniques such as holistic medicine, biofeedback, possibility thinking, psycho- therapy, meditation, hypnosis and a variety of self-im- provement self-help seminars discount the "antiquated, culturally narrow-minded" teachings of the Bible.

The effect of this on many church teachings has been the compromise of Scripture. The Bible is no longer taken seriously and is seen as a culturally irrelevant book with errors. A believer may never be challenged to discover the importance of holiness or acquire a healthy fear of sin or discover the truths of God.

As a young believer, I met a young lady named Linda who shared my desire to know God deeper. One day, Linda invited me over to her parents' home so we could talk about life and God. I brought my Bible, believing we were going to investigate the words of Christ and think of ways we could apply them to our lives.

As we got settled in her living room, she brought out several books by Kahlil Gibran (titles such as, *The Prophet, The Secrets of the Heart, The Broken Wings* and *Spirits Rebellious*). Gibran was a Lebanese poet who was born in Bsherri. After coming to the United States in 1910, he wrote his most famous work, *The Prophet.* This is a long prose poem written in the style of the Old Testament. The story talks about man's philosophical and mystical ability to achieve happiness in his relationship with God, nature and men. To say the least, it was not a companion to the Bible.

There I was, trying to point out truths in the Bible to Linda as she was trying to convince me of the "wonderful" thoughts of Gibran and how his "visions" of insight could help me reach higher to God. Bunk!

The truth is, man's "wisdom" will never discover the reality of the God of our universe. Though man will see His divine nature and eternal power, his wisdom will not honor Him as God (Romans 1:18-21). We must never allow ourselves to be led to believe that our Bible *plus* some philosophical truth of man will lead us to salvation or to a deeper faith in God. Consider Paul's response to the Colossians:

> For in Him all the fulness of Deity dwells in bodily form, and in Him you have been made com-

plete, and He is the head over all rule and authority (Colossians 2:9,10).

Thus:

Set your mind on the things above, not on the things that are on the earth (Colossians 3:2).

2. Legalism (Colossians 2:11-17)

J. I. Packer refers to *legalism* as "a system of requirements" spelled out in a "code or standard of practice" for all situations that, by our observance, operates in some way as a "system of salvation" by which we earn our passage to glory or, at least, "gain a degree of divine favor that we would not otherwise enjoy."[2]

Apparently in the church at Colossae, there were some Jewish legalists who insisted that true salvation required fulfillment of the Old Testament Law that all males be circumcised (Genesis 17:9-14). Paul responded that the Law has been canceled by the "circumcision of Christ" (Colossians 2:11), and that those now in Christ have been buried with Him (and the Law) and also raised up with Him in faith (verse 12). Therefore, we are to let no one or no "law" act as our judge—except the Word of God (Colossians 2:16).

Many times I have seen legalism quench the spirit of a person who desired to know God. Let me tell you about one such incident that I became personally involved in.

A young man named Craig recently joined our fellowship. He is a growing Christian who delights in serving God. He is sincere and genuine with a passion for his Creator. But when he first started to attend our church, he was confused and suspicious about all "organized" churches.

After trusting Christ in his life at a friend's Bible study, he started to attend a small church which seemed to be a stable and friendly group of believers. But this church eventually provoked his anger, confusion and suspicion.

After a few months of attending, Craig started to hear things from the pulpit that did not quite match with what he thought the Scriptures taught. But being a fairly new believer, he did not feel confident enough to approach the leadership with his questions.

One day he got a visit from two of the elders of the church. The visit was friendly and cordial until one of the elders asked Craig about his work and his salary. Being a little surprised by the question but not wanting to offend his guests, he reluctantly told the men what they had asked for. A few minutes later, the elders concluded their visit and were on their way.

A month later, Craig got another visitor from his church—the senior pastor. The visit began with the usual chit-chat until the pastor abruptly asked Craig if he was serious about his love for God. Craig answered with a resounding yes. The pastor then proceeded to tell Craig that the leaders of the church were not sure about his sincerity for God since his tithing receipts were "inconsistent." He told Craig that the church treasurer had observed that his giving was sporadic and often did not add up to 10 percent of his salary. He then challenged Craig to prove his sincerity to God by making a commitment to tithe his weekly salary every Sunday. He added that Craig would never become a strong and mature believer until he consistently gave at least 10 percent.

The pastor's comments angered Craig to the point of leaving the church. For the next five months, he stayed away from every "organized" church, fearing they were only out for his money.

Fortunately, Craig met an old friend who convinced him that most churches are not like the one he left. His friend later brought him by our church and Craig has been growing in our midst ever since.

This story has, in a sense, a happy ending. Even though Craig had been hurt by those misguided believers, he finally was able to understand the fact that there are groups of "believers" who add their legalistic do's and don'ts to the gospel message for the purpose of serving their own beliefs. More often than not, these do's and don'ts have no validity in Scripture.

We must be careful not to allow another believer's personal values or standards (which are not biblically substantiated) to impress on us a particular obligation or duty in our walk with God. When the Romans in Paul's day were arguing about what a "true" Christian should eat, he offered this timeless advice:

> Let not him who eats regard with contempt him who does not eat, and let not him who does not eat judge him who eats, for God has accepted him. Who are you to judge the servant of another? (Romans 14:3,4a)

3. Mysticism (Colossians 2:18,19)

Mysticism is a difficult term to define. It is neither theological nor philosophical and is abstract in its application. But while its definition is elusive, there is a clear difference between the world's view of mysticism and Christian mysticism.

Mysticism outside of Christianity believes that the spirit, through contemplative experience, can be lead to a temporary union of essence with ultimate reality.

Christian mysticism stresses the personal reality of Christ rather than an impersonal "ultimate reality." The union is not one of essence, but the union of human will and love with the reality of God. As a result, such an intimate union shifts a believer's thinking from himself to God. In other words, through deep prayer, meditation or other pious actions, a believer may self-impose humility in order to lead him nearer to the mind and reality of God.

But Christian mysticism can lead to heresy because faulty biblical interpretation results in misapplication. This was the case in the church at Colossae. Apparently, there were some mystics in the church who delighted in false humility (in other words, they were *proud* of their humility). They felt that other believers should worship angels as a means of drawing nearer to the Supreme God because, they boasted, it worked for them.

Paul challenges their false teachings by pointing out that they have separated themselves from the body's head—Jesus Christ. And he adds that growth can only result from God when the entire body is held together by the head. In other words, a believer can experience spiritual growth only through Christ. The worship of angels (or the worship of anything else for that matter), false humility and great visions are not to be pursued in order to grow deeper in our relationship with God.

We must not let anyone hinder our pursuit of God by allowing them to impose their unbiblical ideal of worship and admiration of anything other than Jesus Christ Himself. He is our head and we are His body. He is to be our only source of power and our only point of worship.

4. Asceticism (Colossians 2:20-23)

Asceticism is essentially a philosophy of religious life which centers around the idea of "self-denial" for the purposes of reaching nearer to God.

On the surface, this description may not appear to have any particular faults. But the danger comes in defining "self-denial." Self-denial, in this case, does not refer to a selfless attitude in which we put others before ourselves. Rather, it is referring to denying ourselves physically.

For example, let's say a person chooses to refrain from drinking soft drinks and eating candy bars for as long as he is a Christian. He makes such a commitment because he feels his self-denial will better prove his love for God. Well, denying himself the soda and chocolate bars may be healthy for him, but it will not make him more spiritual or draw him closer to God. It is what is inside him—his spiritual convictions—that will cause him to grow.

Ascetic rules masquerade as a form of piety and religious wisdom. They seem, on the surface, to be reasonable and wise. But what seems to be wisdom is only an appearance of, or pretention to, wisdom. In reality, these rules are expressions of self-imposed worship.[3]

Asceticism and its rules have become the most popular form of working one's way into heaven or into God's good graces. Many people believe that God is only interested in our sacrifice. Nothing could be further from the truth. "For I delight in loyalty rather than sacrifice," declares our God (Hosea 6:6).

God is not interested in our ability to withstand severe physical treatment. He is interested in the faithfulness of our daily walk. He is interested in our inner convictions which prompt us to grow in His Spirit (Galatians 5:16) and in our worship to Him (John 4:23,24).

Our life in Christ will not be enhanced or strengthened by man's philosophies, rules, religious observances and traditions, or self-denial principles. Our strength in Christ can only result from our preparation (seeking forgiveness from sin), our faith (believing the unbelievable), our commitment (consistent loyalty), our attitude (Christ-likeness) and our heart response (a deep reverence for His holiness). These virtues can only be prompted and nurtured by the Word of God—not by the word of any man.

For Reflection, Discussion and Action

1. Before you trusted Christ in your life, did you think that Christianity required a number of additional "weights" to get to heaven?

2. Can you admit to performing any of man's requirements in your Christian life? Are there biblical requirements?

3. What other religions can you name which believe that Christ *plus* something else equals salvation?

4. Can you think of an incident where humanistic philosophy had an effect in your spiritual life?

5. Describe legalism in one sentence. What are you doing now in your Christian life which would be viewed as legalistic?

6. How could Christian mysticism be a benefit to your spiritual life? How could it be a negative influence? Can you name a religion which may appeal to mysticism as its focus in worship?

7. Can you admit to a few practices which could be considered ascetic? How can asceticism contribute to a false sense of humility?

8. Describe what God is looking for in a person who seeks to grow deeper in love with Him.

Part III

Reaching the Goal in His Strength

10

Growing Strong in Our Heart

And give my son Solomon a perfect heart to keep
Thy commandments, Thy testimonies, and Thy
statutes, and to do them all (1 Chronicles 29:19a).

Even with training, it would be foolish for me to set
out on a 100-mile bike ride without first fueling my
muscles with the necessary nutrients for the long ride.
And it would be just as foolish to begin the ride without
carrying extra food and water to use during the trip.

Likewise, it would be naive for us to believe that we
could pursue a deeper relationship with our Creator and
maintain it solely on our own power and resources. Our
strength to grow and endure in the Christian life cannot
be fueled by anything we do. Our only adequate resource
is God's power and might (Philippians 4:13).

How do we utilize His strength in order to continue
our pursuit of a deeper walk with Christ? How do we
keep our eyes focused on His ways? How do we continue
to observe faithfully His truths, which teach us His values
and standards, in an increasingly hostile world? These
are difficult questions to answer. I believe the answers
begin in our heart—the very center of our being, the home

of our deepest intentions, the seat of our emotions (Hebrews 4:12).

You see, you may have made the decision in your *mind* (an intellectual process) to pursue a deeper relationship with God, and you may have proven it to yourself by choosing to read this book. But was it also a response of your heart (your deepest intentions)? Do your heart's convictions and your mental processes both agree that such a pursuit is worthwhile? If both are not in total agreement, your pursuit is destined to lose its motivation as soon as another more challenging or interesting issue grabs your attention.

Does one conviction need to be stronger in order for success? I believe so. Is it our heart response or the response of our intellect? The principle from the Lord's teaching about money answers our question:

> Do not lay up for yourselves treasures upon earth, where moth and rust destroy, and where thieves break in and steal. But lay up for yourselves treasures in heaven, where neither moth nor rust destroys, and where thieves do not break in or steal; for where your treasure is, there will your heart be also (Matthew 6:19-21).

If our heart does not beat for a deeper relationship with God, our mind will not keep us in such a pursuit. But if our heart is in it and our mind is not, I believe, in time, our mind will join the response of our heart. I am convinced that the Bible teaches us that our heart is the driving force in our lives (Hebrews 4:12). It is the biblical symbol for the personality.[1] And it is the place where we can most closely sense the character and reality of God (1 Samuel 16:7; Psalm 44:21; Romans 10:10; 2 Thessalonians 3:5; Hebrews 4:12). Therefore, it is important that we learn how to strengthen our hearts' convictions to maintain our pursuit of God.

Training Our Heart

Strengthening our heart for God is analogous to training for a lengthy bike race. In order for a bicyclist to ready himself, he must reach his "training effect" threshold every time he rides his bike. The "training effect" is the point at which the body improves its ability to adapt to physical stress and overload. Thus, to bring about a training effect, an overload must be applied to the athlete.

As the body adapts to each level or degree of overload, the work must be increased in order to keep bringing about improvements in the athlete's fitness level. If the training loads are not increased, the athlete will simply maintain fitness.[2]

For example, let's say you ride your bike for thirty minutes over the same roads three times a week. Your riding schedule will not improve your fitness. You are merely maintaining your present level.

But let's say for the next ten weeks you ride an additional ten minutes each succeeding week. By the end of the ten weeks you are now riding a total of two hours and ten minutes. You have improved your fitness level by forcing your body to adapt to the increased overload of work created by the additional riding.

This is similar to our relationship with God. The more time and effort we apply in involving God in our thoughts and actions—whether it be through singing, prayer, witnessing or Bible study—the more we train our heart to respond to the things of God.

It's a matter of simply including God in every aspect of our lives—every day. But just as the initial training on a bike may be difficult (depending on how out of shape we are), our initial attempts to include God in all of our ways may be difficult as well (and this, too, will be determined by how far we may have been from God).

But let's back up for a moment. Remember that an athlete must fuel his body with the proper nutrients in order to respond to the increased output of energy required. Likewise, a believer must fuel his heart with a proper measure of spiritual nutrients (faith, purpose, inspiration, etc.) to strengthen his daily thoughts and actions to focus on God. The source of these nutrients is God Himself (2 Thessalonians 2:16,17; Hebrews 13:9).

Then we have to ask: How does a believer draw more of God's nutrients in order to strengthen his ability to dwell daily on Him? And how will this help a believer maintain a consistent pursuit of the very heart of God? I believe the answer to both of these questions centers around the idea of *commitment*:

—a commitment to total *obedience*

—a commitment to *single-mindedness*

—a commitment to *one another in love*

Our Commitment to Obedience

First, let's consider our commitment to obedience. Several years ago, I worked for a short time in a small church. One day, a couple came by my office asking for information about weddings. They wanted to know if they could get married in our church and if we could perform the ceremony. Since my colleague was on vacation, I decided I needed to find out as much about the couple as I could before I committed one of us to begin the pre-marital counseling. (I usually will not commit to performing a marriage ceremony until after the third counseling session.)

The couple was very excited and appeared very

much in love. One of my questions seemed to quench their enthusiasm, though. "Are you both Christians?" I asked. The young man looked at his fianceé then back at me and replied, "I am but she isn't." He went on to explain that they've talked about God, but there was no changing her. She added that she believed Christianity was just another religion and that Jesus Christ was a mortal man—nothing more.

I'd heard statements like hers before and still consented to begin the first three sessions of counseling in the hopes of leading the non-believing partner to Christ. But after that, if there is no interest or a hardened heart on the part of the non-believing partner toward Christ, I will refuse to marry the couple. As a minister of God, I am bound by the Scriptures not to marry a believer to a non-believer (2 Corinthians 6:14).

After hearing the young lady's response, I was compelled to share with the couple what Scripture teaches about the matter. I also shared with them that my call as a minister required that I be obedient to God's Word. But I added that I would begin the counseling sessions.

Upon hearing this, the young man became enraged and told me I had an obligation to marry them regardless. He pointed out that his father was a very generous contributor to our church (of which I was not aware) and that if I didn't marry them, I would later "hear about it." He then stormed out of my office, pulling his fianceé with him.

That evening I received a phone call from this young man's brother. He and I were friends since he was a frequent attender at our church. He told me that I should reconsider my stand. He heard that his father was going to go after me with a bunch of complaints to the church deacons and the senior pastor. I said that I couldn't change my stand because it was more important for me to remain obedient to the Word of God. He then told me as a friend that if I remained unmovable, it would be seen as an embarrassment to his father, and he would most likely do all he could to throw me out of the church. I replied that I did not have a choice in the matter.

Two weeks later, after the senior pastor returned from vacation, I received a phone call from a deacon who asked me to come to an early morning meeting the next day.

At the meeting, I was told of various accusations about my conduct and style of ministry. According to what they had heard, I sparked too many differences between myself and the senior pastor and something had to be done.

I was not given an opportunity to defend myself or respond to the accusations. I felt confused, hurt and alone. Sensing the direction of the meeting, I asked if I could resign.

A few days later I learned that one of the major reasons for the meeting was because I had "willfully" upset a major contributor to our church.

I knew my decision to be obedient to the Scriptures in this matter was going to spark criticism. And I guess I knew that the criticism would be believed since I had not been on staff long enough to prove my character. But still, I never considered compromising the Word of God, nor was my confidence as a proclaimer of His Word shaken. I knew that my utmost responsibility was to uphold the integrity of the Scriptures.

Out of the whole ordeal, God eventually resolved the hurt on both sides. Three years after that incident, the senior pastor wrote me a letter apologizing for the pain he caused, saying that they were not a perfect church but changes were being made. He added that he prays for me from time to time.

Our obedience to God must be total and complete, regardless of the results or circumstances. God is searching for disciples who will be faithful to obey His statutes without question. Such an individual is a disciple who is truly pursuing God with his whole heart. "Blessed are they who keep His statutes and seek Him with all their heart" (Psalm 119:2, NIV).

Our Commitment to Single-mindedness

Single-mindedness simply means to be single focused. Your attention and concentration are aimed totally undistracted in a single direction.

Jesus taught His disciples about the importance of being single-minded. He used money as an illustration:

> No one can serve two masters; for either he will hate the one and love the other, or he will hold to one and despise the other. You cannot serve God and mammon (Matthew 6:24).

James' words about single-mindedness refer to the "unstable ways" of double-minded men. In fact, he wrote about the problems of double-mindedness in two chapters. In James 1:8, he refers to the man who says he believes in God, yet still manifests doubts. This man, he says, will receive nothing from the Lord (James 1:7). In James 4:8, he writes about the believer who attempts to love God *and* the pleasures of the world at the same time. Such a man, he says, must purify his heart:

> Draw near to God and He will draw near to you. Cleanse your hands, you sinners; and purify your hearts, you double-minded.

It's not coincidental that James refers to every believer who is not single-minded as being impure in heart. He is teaching us that as believers we are impure if we allow any other idol or graven image to occupy our hearts. In fact, James reveals several contrasts between good and evil in reference to areas of our Christian life. The conclusion is drawn that the two cannot co-exist without good being defiled by evil (1:6,8,10,26; 2:9; 3:11-12,14; 4:4,8,16).

Thus, if our heart is to grow stronger, it can only do so by being pure. We must be single-minded, focused entirely on God and His Word. Without such a focus, we can never grow in His strength, serve with His motivation or live by His inspiration.

An undivided heart, which worships God alone, and trusts Him as it should, is raised above all anxiety for earthly wants.
—John Cunningham Geikie

Our Commitment to One Another in Love

I find it unfortunate that often I hear believers boast about their close relationship with God while having very poor relationships with their fellow believers. I once knew a man who would stand up in the middle of church business meetings and proclaim that he was walking close to God. Yet everyone in the congregation knew he abused his wife and children, and he had very few close friends—if any.

One cannot read the book of 1 John without clearly understanding the biblical fact that evidence of our love for God reveals itself in our love for one another. In fact, John calls a believer "a liar" if he claims to love God yet hates his brother:

If someone says, "I love God," and hates his brother, he is a liar; for the one who does not love his brother whom he has seen, cannot love God whom he has not seen (1 John 4:20).

The New Testament is full of instructions to us about our treatment of others: Almost eighty verses are attributed to Christ, seventy-four verses to the apostle Paul and twenty-nine verses to various other writers. And all of these instructions center around the element of love (more about this in chapter 12).

In 1 Thessalonians we learn that our love for one another has several powerful by-products, one of which is it strengthens our heart:

And may the Lord make your love to grow and overflow to each other and to everyone else, just as our love does toward you. This will result in your hearts being made strong (1 Thessalonians 3:12,13a, TLB).

Paul's prayer for the Thessalonians is that the Lord will grant them a strong heart in order to be blameless in the presence of God at His return. And an overflow of love is the only way to strengthen one's heart for holy conduct.

As a young Christian, I remember witnessing an overflow of love between two deacons in my church who had finally settled a lengthy feud. After fighting for years over several minor issues, these two men publicly embraced and, with tears streaming down their cheeks, they apologized to each other, to their families and to the church. It made me cry just to watch.

These two men of pride and of power had finally recognized that their feud had only hurt their relationship with God and had nearly split a church. Not surprisingly, from that day on the church began to blossom like never before.

Our love for our fellow man will strengthen our heart for God. After all, if we are truly in love with Him, how could we not love that which He so dearly loves!

I've heard it said that Christian love is at its best when practiced on your neighbor at his worst. If we're truly pursuing a deeper walk with Christ, love for others must begin in our heart so that it can display itself in our home, at our doorstep, at the supermarket, on the road and in our church. As the Lord told His disciples:

> A new commandment I give to you, that you love one another, even as I have loved you, that you also love one another. By this all men will know that you are My disciples, if you have love for one another (John 13:34,35).

For Reflection, Discussion and Action

1. Name some "spiritual" activities that you tend to accomplish on your own without thinking about drawing on God's strength.

2. Do you ever have a conflict regarding an issue that your mind is in favor of but your heart says no? Which response do most people often see from you—your heart response or your mind response? Why?

3. Before you read this chapter, how did you strengthen your heart to stay nearer to God? What things will you do differently now that you've read the chapter?

4. Can you honestly admit to some areas of your life in which you struggle with obedience to God's Word? Can you write them on a piece of paper and commit them to God?

5. What causes your focus on the Lord to become distracted? What do you do to remove the distraction?

6. Would you say that right now you have a close relationship with God? If so, then you are carrying no grudges or complaints in your heart toward another person, right? If that's not the case, will you commit that person to the Lord and promise to settle any negative feelings you have about him or her as soon as possible? If you will, sign your name here _____. Write down the date by which you will settle the matter _____.

Growing Strong in Our Faith

And without faith it is impossible to please Him,
for he who comes to God must believe that He is,
and that He is a rewarder of those who seek Him
(Hebrews 11:6).

George Miller once said, "The beginning of anxiety
is the end of faith, and the beginning of true faith is the
end of anxiety."

Miller's statement implies that there is a *faith*, and
then there is a *true faith*. You'll find support for his belief
in the Bible.

In Matthew 17:14-21, we read about a boy who was
possessed by a demon. The boy was brought before the
disciples who were unable to cast it out. The boy's father
then brought him to Jesus who quickly dispelled the
demon.

After seeing this, the disciples were troubled and
privately asked Jesus why they could not cast out the
demon. Our Lord's answer provides tremendous insight
to the meaning of *true faith*:

And He said to them, "Because of the littleness

127

of your faith; for truly I say to you, if you have faith as
a mustard seed, you shall say to this mountain, 'Move
from here to there,' and it shall move; and nothing
shall be impossible to you" (Matthew 17:20).

Jesus compared effective, true faith to the tiny mustard seed. He was saying that it is not the quantity of our
faith that produces effectiveness, but rather it is the
quality of our faith that produces strength. In other words,
if the amount of our faith is as small as a mustard seed
but based on a deep, sincere trust in God, it is as mighty
as any true faith could be.

Jesus knew the hearts of the disciples. He knew that
they lacked an understanding about true faith. By using
the mustard seed, He taught them that the amount of
faith is not the issue. And by saying the impossible can
be done with faith (like moving a mountain), He was
teaching that the key in displaying the quality of their
faith is seen in how they *live* by it.

For example, someone can say, "I have faith that I
can drive a car." But only the one who has *true* faith will
actually sit in the driver's seat. True faith in God will
exhibit itself in obedient, consistent actions, while a superficial faith (which was apparently the disciples' problem) will only exist as long as there is no trial or
persecution to put it to the test.

Developing True Faith

Now the questions arise: If a person can admit to
having a superficial faith, how can such a faith be
developed into a true faith? How can one's true faith
affect his relationship with God and continue to grow
strong? Let's take a closer look.

If we lift weights, do we develop brand new muscles
or do we build up the ones we have? Obviously we build

up the ones we are endowed with. We do not grow additional muscles.

When a baby is born, he has all the physical features (such as eyes, legs, arms, etc.) that he will have when he is an adult. Apart from maturity, a baby requires no additional features after birth.

Likewise, we have been given all the faith we need at the point of salvation. Developing a deeper faith does not mean that we ask the Lord for additional measures of faith. That was what the disciples meant when they asked the Lord to increase their faith after His instruction to them on the issue of forgiveness (Luke 17:4-6). As we noted earlier, the Lord reminded them that the amount of their faith wasn't the issue. Faith is a gift God gives us because He is saving us (Ephesians 2:8).

Like the weightlifter who must develop his existing muscles and the baby whose existing features develop into adulthood, we must develop and strengthen the faith we have already received from God. We can do this in two different ways: 1. hearing, believing, understanding and living the message proclaimed by the Word of God (Romans 3:22; 4:5; 10:17); and 2. maintaining a daily dependence on prayer (Matthew 17:14-21; Mark 9:17-29).

Knowing the Message Proclaimed by the Word of God

In our world of consumerism and Madison-Avenue marketing, it is becoming more and more difficult to trust products to do what they say they will do. Among other things, we know very little about the true nature of the product in question—other than what we're led to believe.

For example, I recently came across an article critical of a new super fat-soluble vitamin. This vitamin is designed to enhance the body's intake and use of minerals and vitamins. As a result, an athlete's strength and endurance are supposed to be increased so he or she can "overcome the competition."

The article noted that advertisements for this super-vitamin cited two different studies which supposedly supported their claims. Yet, the article pointed out that upon review of the two studies listed in the advertisements, there was no truth to the claim that vitamins strengthen one's endurance at all. One of the studies concluded that there was no evidence whatsoever that indicated mega-doses of vitamins will improve performance. In fact, mega-doses of fat-soluble vitamins were found to be possibly harmful to health and performance.

Instances such as this make it more difficult for the public to trust new products and their advertisements. A good consumer will research a product before he or she trusts it enough to rely on it.

Likewise, the better we know and understand the character of God, the easier it is for us to trust Him. As our reliance on God grows deeper, we become stronger in our faith. It is our increasing knowledge of His ways that strengthens our faith.

Such a truth should not come as any great surprise. Yet it still seems that many believers do nothing more than merely pray a little prayer each day that goes something like, "Oh Lord, give me more faith to follow You!" It is not a matter of quantity, but of knowing and understanding God through His Word (Romans 10:17) and exercising His truths consistently and obediently throughout our life. Only in this way can our faith begin to develop the strength to endure for His glory.

Daily Dependence on Prayer

Andrew Murray was one of the great evangelical leaders of the nineteenth century. He was a man who led a profound devotional life. Influenced by William Law, Murray was a man known for his devotion to prayer and his faith in God. He became one of the most influential evangelical leaders in his generation.

In speaking about faith and prayer, he once wrote:

> Faith needs a life of prayer for its full growth. In all the different parts of the spiritual life there is a close union between unceasing action and reaction, so that each may be both cause and effect. Thus it is with faith. There can be no true prayer without faith; some measure of faith must precede prayer. And yet prayer is also the way to more faith: There can be no higher degrees of faith except through much prayer. This is the lesson Jesus teaches.[1]

Indeed, this is the lesson Jesus teaches. Mark's version of the biblical incident we referred to earlier clearly presents prayer as the foundation for Jesus' ability to cast out the demon:

> And when He had come into the house, His disciples began questioning Him privately, "Why could we not cast it out?" And He said to them, "This kind cannot come out by anything but prayer" (Mark 9:28,29).

The disciples apparently had taken for granted the power they had been given. Consequently, they no longer depended prayerfully on God but operated from their own power. Their failure gave our Lord an opportunity to remind His disciples that prayer was still the primary power behind their faith.

How often we, too, neglect prayer! We become so

focused on results that we neglect the importance of communicating with the Source.

So how and when should we pray? William Law said:

> Be daily, therefore on your knees, in a solemn deliberate performance of this devotion, praying for others in such forms, with such length, importunity, and earnestness, as you use for yourself; and you will find all little, ill-natured passions die away, your heart grow great and generous, delighting in the common happiness of others, as you used to only delight in your own.
>
> For he that daily prays to God, that all men may be happy in heaven, takes the likeliest way to make him wish for, and delight in their happiness on earth.[2]

Prayer and faith are inseparable. Before we ever plan to develop our faith in God, we must first commit our heart to establish a foundation rooted in daily, steadfast prayer.

> He who prays as he should, will endeavor to live as he prays.
> —John Owen

The Marks of True Faith: Endurance

When I read the New Testament, I cannot help but have a sense of awe at the endurance and contentment exhibited by the individuals who lived by their faith— their true faith in God. This resulted from their unshakable confidence in the God of their adoration.

In Hebrews 11, often referred to as the "faith chapter," a number of Old Testament saints are listed whose faith was a testimony to their fellow man as well as a glory to God. The remarkable element in each of the stories is their *endurance*. By relating these stories, the author wants to encourage us not to weaken in the faith in times of persecution. By enduring in the persecution, we can display the fact that our faith is *true* faith.

While it is true that faith means we can rest confidently in what Christ has done for us in the past, it also means we can have complete trust in what He will do for us in the future (Romans 8:12-28; Galatians 3:10-13). We can rest in the fact that regardless of what the future may bring, we can, by faith, trust our God to see us through:

> No temptation has overtaken you but such as is common to man; and God is faithful, who will not allow you to be tempted beyond what you are able, but with the temptation will provide the way of escape also that you may be able to endure it (1 Corinthians 10:13).

This is not to say that we should not expect to experience any suffering. On the contrary, from a biblical perspective, suffering has its place. Most of us wouldn't regard suffering as being good, but it can be a positive experience. The apostle Paul points out that tribulations bring about perseverance and proven character (Romans 5:3-5). The writer of Hebrews reminds us that the disciplines (or trials) of life will yield in us the "peaceful fruit of righteousness" (Hebrews 12:4-11). And James encourages that the trials we encounter serve to test our faith in order to produce endurance (James 1:2-4).

Want to know whether or not your faith in God is true and sincere? Ask yourself what your response was to your last confrontation with persecution or trials. Did your faith weaken? Did you remain silent? Or did you remain steadfast and unmovable? Only you know the condition of the reality of your faith in God. Consider these words of our Lord:

> And you will be hated by all on account of My
> name, but the one who endures to the end, he shall be
> saved (Mark 13:13).

To believe in Christ to the end will require endurance because our faith *will* be challenged. These challenges divide those who display a true faith in God from those who do not. Enduring to the end does not earn salvation for us, but it is a clear mark of those who are already saved. True and sincere faith is a living sign of one who is deeply in love with God.

The Marks of True Faith: Peace and Contentment

Ever watch a Christian in the midst of a difficult trial? If their faith is strong, perhaps the most conspicuous virtue they display is a true sense of contentment, a sense of peace. They understand that God is at work and He is looking out for their best. Therefore, there is simply no need for worry.

After knowing Christ for about a year, I was invited to a Sunday afternoon service operated by several of our church members in a local convalescent home. The service featured a short message, special music and a testimony. At this particular service, something happened that I will never forget.

After the message was delivered, it was time for a testimony. An older man who had lost both of his legs in the attack on Pearl Harbor during World War II raised his hand and asked if he could say something. Without hesitation, we agreed and he quickly rolled his wheelchair to the front.

Ol' Joe began his testimony by sharing that he had been a Christian for thirty-three years. During those years, he had been shuffled a number of times between various retirement homes. Without family or close friends, he had no one to turn to except the Lord . . . and Jesus was his best friend.

Despite his circumstances, Joe never complained. He said that he was perfectly content and at peace with God's plan for his life. He attributed his contentment to his immovable faith in God. He then quoted Philippians 4:11: "Not that I speak from want; for I have learned to be content in whatever circumstance I am."

By this time, most of us were fighting back tears. Here was a man deprived from living what most of us would call a "normal life." Yet his deep and sincere faith in God not only kept him alive, but also fully content and at peace with his maker!

We learned later that Joe's attitude and faith in God had won many to Christ during his stay at the home. The staff referred to him as "the spark of life at the *beginning* of the tunnel." His faith in Christ had not only led several of the residents to Christ, but two of the staff members as well! He was a man whose true faith in God allowed him to endure all those years in difficult circumstances. His faith exhibited such a tremendous sense of peace, joy and contentment that it served as a trophy of God's grace and an inspiration to those he came in contact with.

I often think about Ol' Joe and wonder if he's still alive today. I do know that if he is not on this earth, he's certainly enjoying the riches of heaven.

Joe's case is special, but it isn't that unusual. There are many individuals in Scripture—beginning with Christ—whose true faith in God allowed them to endure persecution and even death with great peace and contentment.

I must admit to feeling a bit guilty when I read or hear about such stories. I still struggle with murmuring and complaining about God's plan for me. Could I display a sense of true peace if it were God's plan that I go through most of my life without the luxury and convenience of two legs? I think most of us still have a lot to learn about the peace and contentment derived from an absolute true faith in our God.

> To believe on Christ is initial faith; to receive Him is appropriating faith; to understand Him is intelligent faith; to assimilate Him is true faith.
> —Cornelius Woelfkin

For Reflection, Discussion and Action

1. Give some examples of faith. Give some examples of true faith.

2. Name some situations in the past which have shaken your faith. What did you do to encourage your faith after these situations?

3. Before reading this chapter, what did you believe a Christian should do to strengthen his or her faith? Had you ever prayed for "more" faith?

4. Before reading this chapter, what did Romans 10:17 mean to you? What does it mean to you now?

5. Will your prayer life change because you've read this chapter? In what ways?

6. Write down some things that you are (or could be) praying about in faith.

Growing Strong in Our Love

But now abide faith, hope, love, these three;
but the greatest of these is love
(1 Corinthians 13:13).

The German poet Heinrich Heine once said, "The deepest truth blooms only from the deepest love."

Heine's statement begins to capture the sentiment behind God's love for us. Only through the deepest truth of His justice, mercy and holiness could He display His deepest love for us through the sacrifice of His Son. His *agape* love was clearly displayed for all mankind. John 3:16 couldn't be more direct:

For God so loved the world, that He gave His only begotten Son, that whoever believes in Him should not perish, but have eternal life.

But how much can man truly understand about God's love? With what kind of love can man respond to God? And can man understand *agape* love outside of Christ? Perhaps we should first consider a biblical definition of love.

Defining New Testament Love

The New Testament uses three different words for *love,* and each word defines a different type of love.

First, there is *agape* love—the love of God. *Agapao* connotes the idea of a deep, sincere, intimate and selfless love—the kind of love Christ displayed for man. A person cannot know and understand *agape* love before he has first realized it through salvation because *agape* love is not purely a human product springing from human resources. It is a result of God's love working in men's hearts.[1]

The second kind of love we find in the New Testament is called *philia.* This word describes the love in a friendship. It implies emotional warmth and attachment leading to a strong affection. Jesus rebuked Peter for having this kind of love for God (John 21:15-17). Peter was rebuked because his love for God lacked the depth of *agape* love.

The third term is *epithymia,* which implies a form of love having a "strong desire." This word is often used to refer to sexual desires or passionate love.[2] A fourth word, *eros* is not found in the New Testament, but is found in Greek literature. It is often linked to romantic sexual love.

It is important that we understand these distinctions because the Bible tells us that our love for God and for one another should be nothing less than *agape* love (Mark 12:30; John 13:34). And yet, often a believer will say he loves God and others when, in truth, his love is nothing more than a strong affection or *philia* love. When we talk about growing strong in our love, we can only be referring to *agape* love. To grow strong in our love means that we move from *philia* love to *agape* love in our response to both man and God.

Growing Strong in Our Love for One Another

Several years ago I read a touching story about the death of Princess Alice. It was written by William Galdstone who had been given the difficult task of announcing her death to the House of Commons.

The little daughter of the princess was seriously ill with diphtheria. The doctors had warned the princess not to endanger her life by kissing her little daughter or breathing the child's breath.

Once when the little girl was struggling to breathe, the mother took her daughter into her arms to keep her from choking to death. Gasping and struggling for her life, the little girl said, "Mama, kiss me!" Without thinking of herself, the mother gently kissed her daughter. As a result, the princess contracted the disease herself and several days later went to be with the Lord.

Princess Alice demonstrated *agape* love. Such a love forgets self. It always puts the needs of others ahead of its own. It is at the very heart of God's immeasurable love for man.

The Bible beautifully describes the reality and application of *agape* love:

> Love is patient, love is kind, and is not jealous; love does not brag and is not arrogant, does not act unbecomingly; it does not seek its own, is not provoked, does not take into account a wrong suffered, does not rejoice in unrighteousness, but rejoices with the truth; bears all things, believes all things, hopes all things, endures all things. Love never fails (1 Corinthians 13:4-8a).

Most believers understand the kind of love 1 Corinthians 13 is referring to. Yet why do we still treat some people with disdain or even hate? Why do we push and shove our way into expressways, ticket lines or even church events without showing love and respect for others? How can we feud with our neighbor and then go to church and sing without guilt, "Oh How I Love Jesus"?

Growing strong in our love for God demands that we grow strong in our love for one another! According to the apostle John: "If someone says, 'I love God,' and hates his brother, he is a liar" (1 John 4:20a).

It must grieve God to listen to our words of praise and love to Him while we harbor hate for a relative or former friend. Don't we understand that it's only by our love for one another that people will know we are disciples of Jesus Christ (John 13:35)? Why is it easier for us to love the "whole" world than to show love to our neighbors by having them over for coffee?

Until we can truly come to the understanding of the awesome depth and power of *agape* love and live it day by day, we will continue to struggle with the ungodly and fleshly feelings of greed, ego, self-pride and self-centeredness—the very drives which prevent us from simply loving others without bias or prejudice. Indeed, the thing that prevents us from totally loving others is our consuming love for ourselves. John Wesley said it best:

> I am sick of opinions. Give me a humble, gentle lover of God and man—a man full of mercy and good fruits, without partiality or hypocrisy. Bigotry is too strong an attachment to our own creed or opinion. How unwilling men are to allow anything good in those who do not agree with them in all things. We must not narrow the cause of God to our own beliefs, but rejoice in goodness wherever it appears.[3]

As a young Christian considering the ministry, I remember a wise and faithful older man of God counseling me about people. He said, "Ron, the church would be a perfect place without people." He was letting me know that ministry wasn't necessarily just spreading the good news from the pulpit and planning fun youth activities. It was working with people. And if I didn't have it in my heart to truly love the unlovable, then I better spend a lot more time in prayer before I apply to seminary.

I must admit that during my fifteen years in the ministry, there have been some situations which have tested my *agape* love for my fellow man. But what has always given me the strength to continue to love despite the most trying circumstances is remembering Christ as He hung on the cross. He looked down upon His scoffers and said, "Father, forgive them; for they do not know what they are doing" (Luke 23:34a). Despite His pain and suffering, He still exhibited love to those who were killing Him! If I am unable to be like Christ, I have no business representing Him in a world desperate for love and compassion.

The most frequent admonition given by the apostles in the early church was to love one another. Paul was perhaps the most direct: "Owe nothing to anyone except to love one another; for he who loves his neighbor has fulfilled the law" (Romans 13:8).

It's interesting that Paul refers to our love for one another as a debt. Compared to the debt that Christ paid on our behalf, our love for one another can never be completely paid up. In other words, there is a continuing debt to love one another since Christ's love for us will always be infinitely greater than ours.

It's easy to say that we "love" the weather or a car or a certain dress. And perhaps it's easy to say that we "love" God. But the reason it's easy is because such love doesn't cost us anything. The most it will probably cost is a weekly attendance at our favorite church.

But the true test of our love is how we treat the

people closest to us. If we have an *agape* love for our
fellow man (who is made in the image of God), we will
treat others as Christ would. Then others will know that
we are "born of God":

> Beloved, let us love one another, for love is from
> God; and every one who loves is born of God and
> knows God (1 John 4:7).

Is your love for your fellow man a *philia* or *agape*
love? Ask yourself the following five questions. If you
have difficulty answering *yes* to any of them, you may
want to ask God to reveal the truth about your deepest
feelings in loving others:

1. Do you often look for opportunities to assist people
   in need, whether or not they are friends or Christians?

2. Can you earnestly love and pray for a person who
   may be openly critical toward you?

3. Would you be quick to help an individual who
   may oppose you at every opportunity?

4. Do your expressions of love toward God and man
   remain the same whether or not you are among
   friends at church or among co-workers on the job?

5. Are others quick to regard you as an individual
   who sincerely cares about others?

Growing Strong in Our Love for God

What does it mean to grow strong in our love for
God? I'd like to quote something I wrote in my first book,
Rediscovering Your First Love:

> Our love relationship with God is not a momen-
> tary emotional experience, but rather a disciplined act

of our will, founded on a deep reverence and submission to a holy and loving God. Such a kinship is the most powerful and dynamic relationship we could ever experience. It is an invincible association with God, who is Himself *love*.[4]

Growing strong in our love for God will become our total motivation in everything we do. It will also produce a pure desire in our hearts to . . .

. . . grow in our obedience to Him (1 John 5:2);

. . . grow in our love for one another (1 John 4:21);

. . . grow in our love for His Word (John 14:23);

. . . grow in our love to serve (2 John 6).

Moving away from merely having a strong affection (*philia*) for God to possessing a deep, intimate *agape* love for Him *will* radically change our lives. Going to church will no longer be an obligation, but an opportunity for worship. Serving the Lord won't be a duty, but a chance for accomplishing a great task for the glory of God. And telling others about the good news of Jesus Christ won't feel like a requirement, but a privilege to communicate the joy in living in peace with our Creator. Indeed, the steps of a truly devoted heart can only proceed in such a way that a radical change in our love and commitment to the Father will be the only result.

Imitating God

Perhaps one of the most difficult and discouraging situations for me in the ministry is working with believers who absolutely refuse to step out of their "comfort zone"—even if there is a tremendous need for them to revitalize their walk with Christ. They continue their "work" for the Lord without desiring to experience a closer, powerful, more intimate relationship with the Father.

That was a problem with the church at Ephesus (Revelation 2), and God rebuked them for leaving their *first love* (verse 4). We, too, can become so "ministry minded" that we easily lose sight of growing "spiritually minded." At that point, we have fallen prey to the erroneous misconception that what counts for the glory of God is what we *do*, not what we *are*.

As a result of such misguided theology, our love for God is born out of a spirit of performance and not out of an internal conviction. Our love becomes methodical and predictable—no stronger than our love for the weather or Grandma's cooking. We now merely have an affection for the Lord. Such a love will never help us endure much sacrifice.

Only an *agape* love can radically change our life in Christ. Henry Drummond declares in no uncertain terms what an *agape* love for God will produce:

> And loving Him, you must become like Him. Love begets love. It is a process of induction. Put a piece of iron in the presence of an electrified object, and that piece of iron for a time becomes electrified. It is changed into a temporary magnet in the mere presence of a permanent magnet, and as long as you leave the two side by side, they are both magnets alike. Remain side by side with Him who loved us, and gave Himself for us, and you, too, will become a permanent magnet . . . and like Him you will draw all men unto you, like Him you will be drawn unto all men. That is the inevitable effect of love.[5]

One of my favorite passages in all the Bible is Ephesians 5:1,2:

> Therefore be imitators of God as beloved

children; and walk in love, just as Christ also loved you, and gave Himself up for us, an offering and a sacrifice to God as a fragrant aroma.

Imagine Paul telling us to imitate God! Being a father, I understand Paul's reasoning. My oldest boy, Ryan, is just turning five. I can't even get out of bed in the morning without him walking in my tracks and imitating my every move. He wants to do everything I do (which is both pleasant and frightening)! So, if love is the essence of the nature of God, then we, as His children, will imitate His love. Love, then, becomes the essential ingredient of the Christian character.

The phrase in Ephesians 5:1,2 which strikes me the most, though, is "walk in love" (verse 2). Too often, I believe we overlook that little word *in*. Paul is telling us not only to imitate our God, but also to be *in love* with God and with our fellow man.

How do you treat someone you are in love with? With kindness? Respect? Sensitivity? Gentleness? We could make a list at least a couple of pages long.

Now how does it strike you to know that God wants us to go about our daily business exhibiting such a character? Feel convicted? I do. But that's exactly what He wants to drive home to us. We are to be imitators of God and walk in love—without any pretensions or conditions.

A Faith of Conviction

I believe it was David Wilkerson who once said that first generation Christians are believers out of conviction; second generation believers are Christians out of belief; and third generation "Christians" are merely believers of an idea.

I am a first generation believer. My children will be

second generation Christians. The thought of that makes me a little nervous. Will they come to Christ because of my belief or out of their own internal conviction? And what about my grandchildren? How will they view Christianity?

You see, people will die for their convictions, but few will die for their beliefs. And no one will die for an idea.

Is our desire to pursue a deep, intimate *agape* love for God a result of an internal conviction? Or is it being encouraged to develop merely out of a belief? Pursuing a true love relationship with our God can only result from a burning internal conviction which serves as a relentless drive in our heart to draw nearer and nearer to Him.

Such conviction caused the apostles and thousands of martyrs since the early church to gladly accept death rather than forsake the Father. Their *agape* love was nurtured in their conviction that Christ Jesus was who He said He was. Therefore, He was worth dying for.

Do you have a sincere conviction to love God, free from conditions or requirements? I'd like to quote once more from *Rediscovering Your First Love*:

> If what we choose to love is God, then He will be our God. We will carry Him in our heart and will honor Him in our ways. So let us choose to fall in love with God. And let our love be faithful and true, for God delights in unchanging love (Micah 7:18). And in our love, let us remember Jude's closing exhortation to the Christians of his day, that we are to keep ourselves "in the love of God, waiting anxiously for the mercy of our Lord Jesus Christ to eternal life" (Jude 21).[6]

Let our conviction be to know God *well* and to walk in love with Him without compromise.

For Reflection, Discussion and Action

1. Before reading this chapter, how would you have defined New Testament love? Could you say that you were freely living it?

2. Give some examples of *philia* love and *agape* love in your life.

3. Why is *agape* love a difficult concept for Christians to grasp in our day and age?

4. Describe an incident in which you did not show *agape* love when you should have. Describe an incident in which you did show *agape* love.

5. Did you answer the five questions on page 142? Which question offers the most challenge to you? Why?

6. Before reading this chapter, how would you have described your love for God? How would you describe your love now?

7. Write down some steps you can take to ensure that you will make a sincere effort to "walk in love."

Notes

Chapter One

1. For a further study on the sin nature of man, see Psalm 51:5; 2 Corinthians 4:4; Ephesians 4:18; Romans 1:18-3:20.

2. William Barclay, "The Letters of James and Peter," *The Daily Study Bible Series* (Philadelphia, PA: The Westminster Press, 1976), p. 192.

3. Brother Lawrence, *The Practice of the Presence of God* (Old Tappan, NJ: Fleming H. Revell, 1981), pp. 62-63.

Chapter Two

1. *The Encyclopedia of Religious Quotations*, Frank S. Mead, editor (Old Tappan, NJ: Fleming H. Revell, 1985), p. 235.

Chapter Three

1. For a good overview of the spiritual gifts, I suggest you read *The Secret* by Bill Bright (Here's Life Publishers, 1989). You'll find Appendix C particularly helpful.

Chapter Four

1. For an in-depth discussion of this topic, I suggest you read my book, *Rediscovering Your First Love* (Here's Life Publishers, 1990).

2. Vernon Grounds, *Radical Commitment* (Portland, OR: Multonamah Press, 1984), p. 42.

3. Grounds, p. 42.

Chapter Five

1. J. Dwight Pentecost, *Things Which Become Sound Doctrine* (Grand Rapids, MI: Zondervan Publishing House, 1980), p. 118.

2. Gary L. McIntosh, "Reaching Baby Boomers, Part I," *Church Growth Network* (1989), p. 3.

Chapter Six

1. Anthony Campolo, *Growing Up In America* (Grand Rapids, MI: Zondervan Publishing House, 1989), p. 203.

2. Campolo, pp. 203-204.

3. For an excellent resource on discipleship, I suggest *Personal Disciplemaking* by Christopher B. Adsit (Here's Life Publishers, 1988).

Chapter Nine

1. For more information, read *The Seduction of Christianity* by Dave Hunt and T. A. McMahon (Harvest House, 1987).

2. J. I. Packer, *Keep In Step With The Spirit* (Old Tappan, NJ: Fleming H. Revell Company, 1984), pp. 112-113.

3. Curtis Vaughan, "Colossians," *The Expositor's Bible Commentary*, Frank E. Gaebelein, editor (Grand Rapids, MI: Zondervan Publishing House, 1978), p. 207.

Chapter Ten

1. Curtis Vaughan, "Colossians," *The Expositor's Bible Commentary*, Frank E. Gaebelein, editor (Grand Rapids, MI: Zondervan Publishing House, 1978), p. 152.

2. "Training Concepts," *Rider Development Clinic Manual* (Colorado Springs, CO: United States Cycling Federation, and Bicycling Magazine, 1990), p. 50.

Chapter Eleven

1. Andrew Murray, *With Christ in the School of Prayer* (Springfield, PA: Whitaker House Publishers, 1981), p. 98.

2. William Law, *A Serious Call to a Devout and Holy Life* (Wilton, CT: Morhouse-Barlow, 1982), pp. 50-51.

Chapter Twelve

1. Leon Morris, *Testaments of Love: A Study of Love in the Bible* (Grand Rapids, MI: William B. Eerdman's Publishing, 1981), p. 41.

2. Morris, p. 119.

3. Walter B. Knight, *Knight's Treasury of Illustrations* (Grand Rapids, MI: William B. Eerdman's Publishing, 1963), p. 213.

4. Ronald F. Bridges, *Rediscovering Your First Love: The Joys of a Devoted Heart* (San Bernardino, CA: Here's Life Publishers, 1990), p. 66.

5. Henry Drummond, *The Greatest Thing in the World* (Springfield, PA: Whitaker House Publishers, 1981), pp. 42-43.

6. Bridges, p. 265.

The Joys of a
Devoted Heart

REDISCOVERING YOUR FIRST LOVE

by Ronald F. Bridges

Discover warm, practical help from a fellow Christian who made the journey back to a vibrant love relationship with God, his family and fellow believers.

Rediscovering Your First Love takes an in-depth look at what loving God really means and the impact that love relationship can have in our lives.

Excellent for group study.

At Christian bookstores everywhere.
Or call

The Incredible Power
of Intercessory Prayer

DON'T JUST STAND THERE, *PRAY SOMETHING*

by Ronald Dunn

In one of the most helpful books on prayer ever written, Ronald Dunn teaches you how to pray more effectively for your personal needs, for the needs of others, and for national revival.

Includes free bonus section, "How to Start an Intercessory Prayer Ministry in Your Church."

At Christian bookstores everywhere.

Or call